THE ULTIMATE
KOGIN
COLLECTION

Projects and patterns for
counted sashiko embroidery

Susan Briscoe

sewandso

www.sewandso.co.uk

CONTENTS

INTRODUCTION

Kogin (from the western part of Aomori Prefecture), Nanbu hishizashi (a close relative from eastern Aomori) and Shōnai shashiko (from western Yamagata Prefecture) are said to be the three great sashiko traditions from Tohoku (northern Japan). Kogin and Nanbu hishizashi are counted thread embroideries, while Shōnai sashiko is not counted. All have long traditions and have had modern revivals.

I began my Japanese stitching adventures after working in Shōnai as an English teacher in the early 1990s, and this led to the publication of *The Ultimate Sashiko Sourcebook* in 2005. Lessons with Keiko Abe in Yuza-machi in Shōnai, and later with Yoko Sato in Hirosaki, started my passion for kogin, but this different technique demanded another book!

In this book, I have collected over 230 traditional patterns for kogin and Nanbu hishizashi, with advice on the tools and materials needed and step-by-step instruction for all the basic techniques. There's a selection of projects for you to explore, from simple to more complex pieces, playing with traditional and contemporary styles. But first, let's start our kogin journey with a look at its fascinating history.

THE ORIGINS OF KOGIN

Kogin embroidery originates from the Tsugaru region, in and around Hirosaki city in the north of Honshu, Japan's largest island. With running stitches in white cotton thread on dark indigo *asa* cloth (made from hemp or other bast fibre), kogin is said to resemble snow scattered on the ground. It is stitched from side to side, counting over mostly uneven numbers of threads: one, three, five and, very occasionally, seven. Long stitches, avoided on the front of the cloth, may be present on the back, resulting in fabric almost three times its original thickness, trapping air for warmth. The original *asa* cloth was quite fine and woven with more warp than weft threads, traditionally 13–14in (33–35.6cm) wide, which slightly elongated the patterns vertically into the characteristic diamond shapes.

The name 'kogin' comes from *koginu* (*ko* = small, *ginu* = wear), the name of a long jacket with a centre back seam similar to a *hanten* (work jacket). Kogin was also used on *sodenashi* ('sleeveless' waistcoats), although few have survived. Kogin was first recorded in the Genroku era (1688–1704), but the first image of a woman wearing a *sashiko-ginu* (kogin sashiko wear) jacket, does not appear until 1788 in *Ōmin-zui*, a book written by Hirano Sadahiko, an employee of the Tsugaru Han residence in Edo (now Tokyo). Although no stitched examples of kogin exist from that time, we do know that the three regional styles - *Higashi* (east), *Nishi* (west) and *Mishima* (three stripe) - were already established, as Hirano illustrated them all. The illustrations show kogin extending onto the jacket sleeves and one with it all over the body, although the earliest museum examples dating from the first half of the 19th century rarely have kogin stitched anywhere other than the bodice. The unembroidered sleeves, lower 'skirt' sections and collars could be replaced as they wore out and the kogin bodice recycled into a new garment; in fact, only the bodice has been preserved from many antique kogin jackets. Originally stitched as 'Sunday best' and festival attire, worn-out garments were demoted to everyday wear, sometimes with extra vertical stitching called *niju-sashi* (twice stitched) kogin added to reinforce tattered sections; others - *somekogin* (dyed kogin) - were over-dyed with indigo to hide discolouration.

Illustration of woman and child included on the cover of the fabric shade card from Hirosaki-based shop, Tsukiya, adapted from the book Ōmin-zui. Girls were taught simple kogin from six years old, progressing to more complex patterns from age ten, and teenage girls began to make kogin trousseau for future family life.

Example of antique kogin: new kogin was worn for best, but as it became worn and repaired, it was relegated to everyday wear.

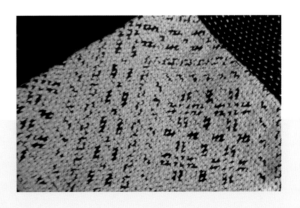

Detail of niju-sashi (twice stitched) kogin: this technique, while extending the life of the garment, often obscured the original stitching pattern.

TRADITIONAL KOGIN FABRIC AND THREAD

Sumptuary regulations of the Edo era (1603–1868) affected what could be consumed, and the Frugality Act for Farmers (1724) prohibited peasants from buying or using cotton or silk cloth, so hemp, ramie, nettle and other bast fibres were their only options. Hemp was grown to make fabric for clothes, sacks, futon covers and mosquito nets, in addition to other items, and it was woven at home. Newly spun hemp thread was very rough, but by boiling the woven cloth in lye, exposing it to the sun and soaking it repeatedly in cold water, it could be softened.

Sun-bleached hemp and ramie cloth was dyed with home-grown *tadeai* (dyer's knotweed), or with indigo by the local dyer, the only bought dyestuff farmers were permitted to wear (indigo strengthens the fibres and the smell of natural indigo was thought to repel snakes and insects). After dyeing, fabric was then further softened, by beating it with a wooden mallet.

In order to try to keep their families warm during Tsugaru's long, snowy winters, women initially stitched kogin using hemp thread to thicken and strengthen the woven hemp cloth. From 1791, however, the feudal government began to promote weaving with cotton grown further south in Japan, and kogin stitchers switched to cotton thread. Cotton thread covered the woven hemp very well, giving the kogin a pleasingly dense yet delicate appearance, but although it was warmer to wear, several layers still had to be worn to keep out the cold.

The railway came to Hirosaki in 1894–1895, contributing to the decline of kogin as mass-produced fabrics became more readily available (sumptuary regulations having been abolished with the Meiji Restoration in 1868). According to kogin teacher and author Setsu Maeda, kogin reached its peak in the decade immediately prior to the railway's construction, with eight out of ten women stitching it.

Mount Iwaki, popularly called 'Tsugaru Fuji'. Kogin's densely worked stitching helped to keep the peasant farmers warm during Tsugaru's long, cold winters.

HIROSAKI CITY AND KOGIN

Hirosaki (the city at the heart of the region where kogin originated) developed as the castle town of the Tsugaru Han (Tsugaru feudal domain), ruled by the Tsugaru clan, rivals of the neighbouring Nanbu clan who had previously held the area from the late 12th century. Oūra Tamenobu, founder of the Tsugaru Han, was originally a retainer of the Nanbu clan, but allied himself with Tokugawa Ieyasu, founder of the Tokugawa Shogunate, which unified and ruled Japan from 1603 until the Meiji Restoration in 1868.

Apple horticulture was introduced to the Hirosaki area in 1877, and Aomori Prefecture is now the main apple producer in Japan. Hirosaki was awarded city status in 1889 and its emblem is the Buddhist *manju*, a symbol that can be seen in *sayagata* (saya brocade). The areas where kogin was stitched are quite close to each other, and places that were once villages are now suburbs of Hirosaki city. As well as its kogin traditions, Hirosaki is also known for its cherry blossom festival, the production of Tsugaru Nuri lacquerware, and nearby Mount Iwaki.

The castle at Hirosaki, built in the early 17th century by Oūra Tamenobu, founder of the Tsugaru Han.

The sayagata (saya brocade) pattern features the Buddhist manju, which is the emblem of Hirosaki city.

Aomori Prefecture (shaded green here) lies at the northern tip of Honshu island, Japan.

Mishima kogin

Aomori city

TSUGARU

Higashi kogin

Nishi kogin

Hirosaki city

NANBU

Nanbu hishizashi

Detail of Aomori Prefecture showing the three regional areas of kogin and the Nanbu hishizashi area.

Three koginu illustrating the regional styles of kogin. Koginu were unlined and did not have the overlap panels at the front opening seen on kimono today. Patterns had to be matched up carefully on each side and across a centre back seam. The sleeves could be long and square like kimono, or tapered for work like hanten. (Originally stitched as 'Sunday best' and festival wear, the hanten sleeves may be later alterations when garments were recycled as work clothes.)

Higashi (east) kogin, front.

Higashi (east) kogin, back.

Nishi (west) kogin, front.

Nishi (west) kogin, back.

Mishima (three stripe), front.

Mishima (three stripe), back.

REGIONAL STYLES

Kogin's three distinctive regional styles are displayed on a set of jackets, re-created in miniature by the Kogin Lab (a Hirosaki-based institute dedicated to preserving traditional kogin). Young women marrying and moving to their husbands' homes would have spread kogin patterns from village to village.

Higashi (east) kogin: From the area around the Iwaki River, the castle district and Ishikawa region of Hirosaki city, and Kuroishi city and Hirakawa city on the east side. It has an all-over repeat pattern, same front and back, stitched continuously on roughly woven cloth. Complex patterns have very large motifs made with multiple borders; others include vertical columns of motifs, occasionally with a little variation between left and right panels on the jacket front; and a few are a sampler of kogin patterns. Particularly popular was the *sayagata* (saya brocade) pattern, representing prosperity and longevity.

Nishi (west) kogin: From the area west of Hirosaki, including Nishi-ya village, Hirosaki city's Iwaki district, Soma area and across the Iwaki River. There are three pattern bands on the front and two on the back. Narrow bands of running stitch called *shima* (stripes) cross the shoulders, stitched alternately with white and black threads, and dividing the patterned bands in white thread, so it is sometimes called *shima* kogin. The simple shoulder bands were very hard-wearing when carrying heavy loads. The first pattern band directly below the shoulder area often featured *sakasakobu* (inverted patterns), said to be a charm against snake bites. The fabric is finely woven and Nishi kogin was considered to be the best, so skilled stitchers were sought after in marriage.

Mishima (three stripe) kogin: From the area north of Hirosaki, around Kanagi town near Goshogawara city. Farms were poorer here, as much of the land was peat moor: life was very hard and few women could invest the time to excel at kogin, and few antique *koginu* remain. However, the Sanaburi Arauma festival, taking place in early summer in Kanagi, when the god of the rice fields goes out on horseback, has preserved kogin in the horse-keeper's costume. The three main pattern bands on front and back are separated by wide bands of white and black stitches, with a smaller pattern on the shoulders. The pattern bands have multiple designs arranged in large V-shapes, which create a W-shaped design across the back. Patterns either side of the back panel are usually the same, but left and right front panels often differ.

THE ORIGINS OF NANBU HISHIZASHI

Although similar to kogin, Nanbu hishizashi is not strictly speaking one of the kogin traditions. Originating in the Nanbu area in eastern Aomori Prefecture about 200 years ago, it is stitched over even numbers of threads, which gives the patterns their distinctive sideways diamond shape (*hishizashi* means 'diamond stitch'). Nanbu hishizashi can't be integrated directly with kogin patterns because the diagonal 'step' is different, but it is sometimes combined on the same panel in modern work (see Projects: Table Runner).

The climate of the Aomori Prefecture had a part to play in the development of the Nanbu hishizashi tradition. Unlike Tsugaru in the west, which was a rice-growing area with a wet climate, Nanbu was drier with little snowfall and frequent crop failures, so farmers were poorer. The *hishi* (diamond) motifs express a wish for increasing prosperity while the points of the diamonds were believed to stab evil. *Katako* (small shape patterns) is the name given to the basic Nanbu hishizashi diamond motifs. There are also continuous patterns.

Makanai *jacket shoulder area detail, stitched in indigo with characteristic* hisihi *(diamond) motifs.*

Jackets, called *makanai*, which could be worn for almost any occasion, were stitched with dark indigo on natural or very pale indigo hemp fabric, often woven at home. They had comparatively tight sleeves with underarm gussets and were mainly stitched on the shoulders or the top of the sleeves, sometimes both, and occasionally all over. Hishizashi patterns were also combined with *hitomezashi* (one stitch) sashiko patterns and simple horizontal stitched rows. *Tattsuke* (women's tight pants, like leggings) were stitched in wide bands, alternating between white and dark indigo thread, from ankle to mid thigh and sometimes right up to the waist.

The arrival of the railway to Aomori Prefecture in 1894-1895 gave the young women stitchers access to exotic woollen yarn. The multicoloured *maedare* (aprons with three panels), stitched in wool and later synthetic threads, expressed a joyful use of colour that is unique in sashiko traditions. These aprons were made until the mid-20th century, but their heyday was the Taisho era (1912-1926). Worn for festivals and as 'Sunday best', colour changes, rather than different stitch patterns, create the design, usually arranged to make larger diamonds, zigzags or the diagonal hashtag design called *igeta* (well curb).

Nanbu hishizashi makanai *jacket and* tattuske *pants (The Amuse Museum, Tokyo).*

A multicoloured maedare *for which Berlin woolwork thread was often used. Hishizashi was confined to the apron's central panel with the top 6-8in (15-20cm) usually worked in sashiko.*

Detail from a maedare *panel.*

KOGIN REVIVAL

In 1932, Muneyoshi Yanagi (1889–1961), better known outside Japan as Sōetsu Yanagi, the founder of the Japanese *Mingei* (People's Art) movement, wrote in *Kōgei* (*Crafts*), the journal of the Japanese Folk Arts Association: 'It must have been sad to face the snow-bound life in winter as one's fate, but people's cursing against their fate is not reflected in kogin. What is reflected is the joy of their creation.' In 1936 he established the *Nihon Mingeikan* (Japan Folk Crafts Museum) in Tokyo, which has many examples of kogin.

Kogin teacher Setsu Maeda also visited the USA and Europe to spread kogin stitching techniques overseas.

Kogin began to be re-evaluated in Tsugaru too. The collector and designer Teizo Soma (1908–1988) of Hirosaki city was an associate of Yanagi. After graduating from university, he returned to Tsugaru and organised many exhibitions of local crafts, establishing a local branch of the Japanese Folk Arts Association and becoming Director in 1942.

Another important figure was kogin artist and teacher Setsu Maeda (1919–1995). Born in Goshogawara city, she was taught kogin by Tokuko Kudo and went on to found the *Kogin Murasaki Kai* (Kogin Purple Circle Association) and to teach kogin to adults and children in Hirosaki. Kogin was classed as *Mukei Bunkazai* (Important Intangible Cultural Property) and was included in school handicraft lessons. Maeda wrote several books, including two called *Tsugaru Kogin Zashi*, published in 1981 and 1983. She described kogin as '"wisdom for living" created by our forefathers, to be handed down from generation to generation.'

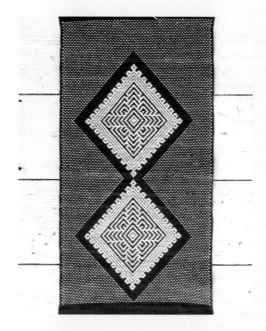

"The original type of kogin, pieced of blue linen with designs in white cotton threads, represents one of the great beauties of folk arts. It is, however, one of our subjects to create the new works of kogin which more fits in well with the life of today."

Setsu Maeda (1919-1995) from Tsugaru Kogin Zashi, *published in 1983.*

Partly stitched project from a design published in Tsugaru Kogin Zashi (1981) by Setsu Maeda, bought in a Japanese flea market. Extending and combining traditional patterns in new ways was a hallmark of her popular designs.

HIROSAKI KOGIN LAB

Originally founded as Hirosaki Home Spun Ltd in 1942 by Naomichi Yokoshima, it changed its name to Hirosaki *Kogin Kenkyū-jyo* (Kogin Laboratory or just Kogin Lab, also translated as 'Kogin Institute') in 1962, with Naomichi becoming the first Chief Executive Officer (CEO). Kogin Lab is dedicated to preserving traditional kogin and promoting it as a living craft technique to be enjoyed by future generations.

Believing it to be their social responsibility to inherit and cherish traditional kogin, Kogin Lab's staff interviewed local people in their homes, collecting antique kogin clothes and materials, copying the kogin patterns onto graph paper and confirming the patterns by laboriously reproducing the stitching.

Kogin Lab realised that kogin could become obsolete unless it was reinvented to make products people wanted to buy, without compromising on traditional materials and techniques. Hiroko Takahashi (nee Kosugi, 1925-2015) worked there from its beginning to 1956, learning kogin from Naomichi and Haru Yokoshima and then from Kazutomo Takahashi, whom she married in 1970: he produced many kogin patterns as graph paper charts, which she stitched.

Traditional designs are given a modern application in Hirosaki Kogin Lab items, sold throughout Aomori Prefecture and at special events showcasing regional products throughout Japan.

'Gestures in Clothing' exhibition, Aomori Contemporary Art Centre, 2013

This exhibition by Osaka-based artist OH Haji, quoted below, incorporated many items from the collection of the archives of the Keikokan Museum (now held by Aomori City Council since the museum's closure in 2006).

"Kogin is said to have been passed down and worn across generations. When looking at *somekogin* (dyed kogin), we can see just how much one kogin was cherished; kogin that began as someone's Sunday best turned into everyday clothing and finally to work clothing, unravelled and re-stitched many times in the process. A unique softness also appears from beating after washing and dyeing. Gestures in the clothing remain vivid as evidence of their owner's years of hard work. *Somekogin* made of ramie have gained a black lustre and flexible texture. The dirty and frayed remnants, patchwork of *niju-sashi* (twice stitched) kogin, and deep blue hue of *somekogin* are the evidence of daily labour, and we can also say that they are the evidence of someone's life. Naturally, these traces are not made intentionally, but they possess a value incomparable with anything else... The immense task of producing clothing, which began with planting the seed, was the accumulation of tremendous toil, but there must have been joy and amusement in the creation and inheritance of various patterns over generations. Indeed, vivid scenes are recorded where friends and peers would get together to vie with each other for the best stitch."

*An assortment of small items
created by Kogin Lab.*

Today, Kogin Lab acts as a hub for the manufacture and sale of kogin products, employing around 100 kogin stitchers. The kogin they produce is made up into accessories and household items, often with a very modern application, such as credit card cases or key rings, as well as larger items. Every year, around 3,300 yards (3,000 metres) of hemp cloth is specially woven, to the correct thread count and free of irregularities, and dyed in Shiga Prefecture for Kogin Lab's exclusive use. As well as the traditional white on indigo, other fabric and thread colour combinations are employed, to appeal to modern tastes. Sadaharu Narita, who became the third CEO in 1982, described in an interview with Tohoku Standard - an online platform that promotes products and traditions from Tohoku region - how the geometric patterns of kogin have international appeal. An infinite number of different things can be made from the same basic units, and he believes it is important to pass these patterns down as accurately as possible.

Kogin teacher Yoko Sato, a former pupil of Setsu Maeda, opened a kogin gallery at her home in 2010, where she displays her work as a teacher and also work by her original inspiration, Hiroko Takahashi, who stitched many early samples for Kogin Lab.

CHUZABURO TANAKA'S COLLECTION

Folklorist and archaeologist, Chuzaburo Tanaka (1933–2013) was born in Aomori Prefecture and collected around 30,000 items, including kogin, Nanbu hishizashi, *boro* (rag patchwork), and Jōmon era (14,500–300 BCE) pottery (interestingly, the diamond and zigzag patterns of kogin are similar to pottery designs of this era). Tanaka spent over 40 years visiting rural areas, studying and collecting garments and tools from elderly people who entrusted their treasures and stories to him.

From 2009–2019, part of Tanaka's collection was displayed at the Amuse Museum, Tokyo, a 'live museum' that encouraged visitors to touch and experience the exhibits in unique, immersive displays. In addition to the permanent galleries, where exhibits were displayed in rotation, there have been many 'special exhibitions' focusing on different parts of the collection, such as Nanbu hishizashi *tattsuke* (women's tight pants, like leggings) in 2010, Nanbu hishizashi *maedare* (aprons) in 2014, and kogin in 2018.

Detail of a maedare (apron) panel from Tanaka's collection, displayed at the Amuse Museum, Tokyo, from 2009–2019. The collection is considered extremely important in understanding Japan's clothing culture providing inspiration to many, including director Akira Kurosawa, who collaborated with Tanaka to use original Nanbu hishizashi clothing in the film Dreams.

An example of a large medallion sampler panel of the sort that became popular in the late 20th century, from Chuzaburo Tanaka's collection at the Amuse Museum.

KOGIN BOOKS AND MODERN MATERIALS

Books have been important for the popularity of kogin in Japan. Naomichi Yokoshima's research at the Kogin Lab resulted in the publication of *Kogin* (1966) and *Tsugaru Kogin* (1974), which was published in a revised and extended edition with many new illustrations as *Tsugaru Kogin Zashi* in 2013, with two copies being donated to every Japanese prefectural library service. Yokoshima's books present kogin in a very traditional style, mostly illustrated with stitched examples rather than charts on graph paper.

In the early 1960s, *Kogin Toge Shisū* (Kogin Embroidery), a series of three books written by Kikuko Miyake, included projects and charted patterns, introducing new colour combinations and materials. Miyake's project ideas included contemporary items such as a magazine rack, sofa back covers, a piano top valance, aprons for barbecue wear, modern handbags and fashions, and even a television screen cover, alongside kimono, *obi* (kimono sashes), tea ceremony items, cushions, screens and other pieces for traditional interiors. This approach of using kogin for items appropriate for modern living has continued to the present day; some designers are even creating new patterns in kogin, or mixing in other pattern darning traditions, such as Norwegian *smøyg*.

Getting hold of traditional kogin materials outside of Aomori Prefecture seems to have been an issue for Japanese readers in the 1960s, as these early books show a selection of different fabrics and threads suitable for kogin.

"Although kogin is an old thing rooted in tradition, it is easy for anyone to have kogin's beauty in their lifestyle today. The previous book's collection highlighted the original (traditional) beauty of kogin, but this time I will use my mind to express a modern kogin style."

Kikuko Miyake, from the introduction of the second volume of Kogin Toge Shisū.

Kogin Toge Shisū (*Kogin Embroidery), a series of three books by Kikuko Miyake.*

Kogin books of the 1950s and 60s were packed with projects showing kogin used for fab and funky modern fashions and homes, alongside traditional items.

Meeting the needs of modern kogin stitchers, Olympus introduced threads in many colours, followed by kogin kits with everything required.

A reversible obi *stitched using Olympus thread by Keiko Abe, who adapted the pattern from* Shin Kogin Shishū Nyūmon *by Misao Kimura, published in 1991. (Kimura exhibited in the USA in 1963.)*

When Hanamura, a kogin materials supplier based in Hirosaki, closed in 2000, former manager Takayoshi Takeuchi opened *Tsukiya*, a needlework shop specialising in kogin now run by his son, Takashi Takeuchi. Several other craft shops sell kogin materials in the area, but specialist suppliers are very localised. In response to wider demand, the craft company Olympus started producing kogin thread and fabric from 1955, introducing kogin kits in 1978, now sold internationally. Popular materials for kogin include 18-count and 20-count evenweave embroidery fabrics, in cotton and linen (see Tools and Materials).

CURRENT TRENDS IN KOGIN

New books on kogin are published annually in Japan, and many stitchers share their work on the internet. The largest kogin event is Kogin Fes, first held in 2011, an exhibition and festival that takes place annually in Hirosaki at the end of April. It attracts many exhibitors and traders, displaying antique and contemporary kogin and Nanbu hishizashi. In addition to the traditional white on blue, a lot of modern kogin is stitched on light coloured fabric with colourful threads, which is easier to see while stitching. Natural linen is popular, even stitched with white thread for a very subtle look. At the seventh Kogin Fes in 2018, many traders had shaded and naturally dyed threads for sale, including Ringoworks, a local company that dyes thread and fabric using apple leaves and bark, by-products of regional apple farming. Alongside small quick-to-make projects, there were also many larger works to be seen, such as the indigo stencilled kogin panels made by Toshiaki Tanaka, combining the art of *katazome* (stencil dyeing) with kogin. Three hundred years on, kogin and Nanbu hishizashi look set to continue, as each generation brings their own interpretation to these traditions.

Toshiaki Tanaka combines kogin with traditional katazome stencil dyeing. He uses a tapestry frame to stab stitch his calligraphy designs, which include very long stitches.

TOOLS AND MATERIALS

You need only basic sewing equipment to stitch kogin and, if you are a stitcher already, you are likely to have everything you require at hand (see Basic sewing kit). If you are keen on a counted thread embroidery technique, such as cross stitch, you may even have some fabric and threads you can use for your first attempts. If you want to invest in fabric, thread and needles specially made for kogin, these are readily available online (see Suppliers). Any specific tools called for to assemble a project will be listed at the start of the project.

TIP

A rotary cutter, quilter's ruler and cutting mat are useful for accurately cutting out backing and lining fabrics.

Basic sewing kit

- ▶ Small embroidery scissors
- ▶ Dressmaking scissors
- ▶ Pins
- ▶ Tacking (basting) thread
- ▶ Sewing sharps
- ▶ Thimble (optional)
- ▶ Iron
- ▶ Marking pens and pencils
- ▶ Tape measure and ruler
- ▶ Sewing machine

NEEDLES

Kogin needles, like cross stitch or needlepoint needles, have a rounded tip to avoid piercing the fabric, but are slightly longer. Some kogin stitchers prefer to use shorter cross stitch needles. The type of needle you use is up to you, so long as it has a blunt tip and an eye large enough to get your preferred thread through your chosen fabric without distorting the weave.

The coin thimble

Traditional kogin stitchers use a *tekka* (coin thimble). They rest the eye end of the long needle on the coin thimble, worn at the base of their middle finger, and scoop the fabric onto the tip of the needle in a similar way to sashiko stitching, where the fabric is pleated onto the needle tip, gathered up and eased out. This traditional technique can feel very unnatural to non-Japanese stitchers and it is all too easy to pull the thread too tight, causing the kogin stitch to sink into the fabric and making stitches over single threads almost disappear (see Basic Techniques: Stitching Kogin, steps 5 and 6 for how to avoid this).

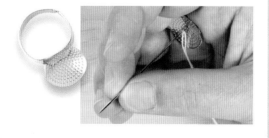

FABRICS

To stitch any counted thread embroidery, you need to be able to easily count the threads that make up the weave of the fabric. Embroidery fabrics sold for kogin have a clearly visible weave so that you can see where to stitch.

Traditionally, kogin and Nanbu hishizashi were stitched on hemp fabrics with a quite fine uneven weave, with a higher number of warp (vertical) threads than weft (horizontal) threads, about 25 threads to the inch (2.5cm). This gives the patterns a slight vertical distortion, emphasising the diamond shape, as seen in many of the items featured in the history section (see Introduction). Cotton and linen fabric with the same uneven weave in different thread counts is sold in Hirosaki today – available by mail order in Japan, but not currently sold abroad. The hemp fabric woven specially for Kogin Lab is not available for sale to other stitchers.

Modern kogin is more widely stitched on evenweave fabrics made from cotton and linen, or sometimes wool, giving the patterns a squarer appearance. The fabrics most popular today are 18-count and 20-count evenweave fabrics; using a lower thread count makes the patterns larger and the stitches longer, so if you do want to try 16-count and 14-count evenweave fabrics, these are best kept for projects where the stitches can't be snagged in use. For Nanbu hishizashi, which includes stitches up to ten threads long, fabric with a higher thread count is preferable to avoid very long stitches, so choose from 20-count upwards. The projects and samples in this book were mostly stitched on 18-count evenweave cotton and 20-count evenweave cotton and linen, with higher count fabrics used for the button project.

One important thing to consider is that the fabric count only refers to the number of threads per inch and not the thickness of those threads, so some fabrics with the same thread count may have a more open weave than others: compare, for example, the 20-count linen used for the linen drawstring bag (see Projects: Drawstring Bags) with the 20-count cotton used for several of the coasters (see Projects: Coaster Collection). So both fabric count and thickness should be taken into consideration when selecting your kogin thread (see Threads).

In addition to kogin and embroidery fabrics, some furnishing fabrics can be suitable for kogin, and you may be able to find weaves that are similar to the traditional uneven weave kogin cloth, which will give kogin an elongated appearance. Look for fabrics where the weave is easy to see, is regular (significant weft unevenness would distort your pattern) and free from large slubs. You may have to make some stitch samples to find the best thread and fabric combinations.

TIP

When choosing fabric for lining and backing the projects, medium-weight cottons used by quilters are ideal, available in many different patterns and colours.

For the fabric samples below, the thread count is indicated by the hashtag sign (#).

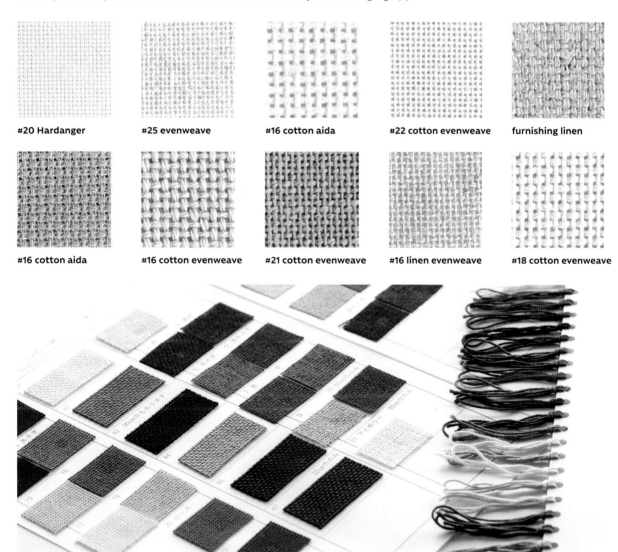

#20 Hardanger   **#25 evenweave**   **#16 cotton aida**   **#22 cotton evenweave**   **furnishing linen**

#16 cotton aida   **#16 cotton evenweave**   **#21 cotton evenweave**   **#16 linen evenweave**   **#18 cotton evenweave**

Thread and fabric samples from Tsukiya, a specialist needlework shop in Hirosaki city.

THREADS

The thread you choose should cover your chosen fabric well, without gaps between rows, if you want to achieve the traditional kogin look. Finding the right balance between thread thickness and fabric count is key. Experiment by stitching up samples of different threads on different fabrics to find what looks best.

Kogin thread: This is a cotton thread that has quite a loose twist, rather like a thicker version of sashiko thread. Several different thicknesses of traditional thread are available in and around Hirosaki and by mail order within Japan. Elsewhere in the world, kogin stitchers will find it easy to source Olympus kogin thread, a six-strand cotton thread that can be split and recombined for excellent fabric coverage on 18-count and 20-count fabrics. It is similar to six-strand embroidery cotton (floss), but a little thicker and without the sheen, and it is available in more than 35 different colours. I used Olympus kogin thread for all the samplers in the Pattern Library and for many of the projects.

Sashiko thread: Olympus sashiko thread is ideal for working on finer fabrics with a higher thread count, but is a little too fine to cover fabrics with a thread count of 20-count or less.

Soft cotton: This thick embroidery thread, more commonly used for needlepoint, is excellent for stitching kogin, especially on 16-count and 18-count evenweave cotton. The kogin on the natural linen drawstring bag (see Projects: Drawstring Bags) was stitched with soft cotton on 20-count linen. Available in more colours than Olympus kogin thread, it does need to be slightly untwisted as you stitch, otherwise the appearance will be stringy. Skeins are 10⅞yd (10m) long.

Stranded cotton (floss): This six-strand thread covers well on 20-count and higher thread counts, and it may be split for working on very high thread counts.

Cotton perle: This is less suitable as it does not tend to spread out to fill the stitch, but it can be successful on some finer fabrics.

Cotton knitting yarn: Some can work well for kogin – double knitting (DK/worsted) is good for 16-count evenweave and 4-ply (sport weight) for 20-count evenweave – but as different brands tend to be slightly different thicknesses, you will need to experiment.

Variegated thread: In recent years, kogin colour trends have seen a rise in the popularity of hand-dyed variegated threads, produced in small quantities and available only in Japan. However, similar threads can be found outside Japan, such as the 4-ply variegated cotton used for the table runner (see Projects: Table Runner). Variegated threads with highly contrasting colour or value (light to dark) variations and/or very short 'pitch' (colour change) length can break up more elaborate kogin patterns, so are best kept for simpler designs.

Woollen thread: If you want to explore stitching Nanbu hishizashi patterns with woollen thread, try tapestry wool for 18-count or 20-count evenweave fabric and crewel wool for finer weaves, but remember, woollen thread is not as hard-wearing as cotton thread.

Olympus threads, sashiko (left) and kogin (right).

Medium sashiko thread covers better on 22-count evenweave (left) than on 18-count evenweave (right).

BASIC TECHNIQUES

The technique for stitching kogin is relatively simple – patterns are created with running stitch going back and forth horizontally across the fabric – and this chapter has all the advice you need to achieve the best possible results, from start to finish. Kogin patterns are usually stitched from charts, so that's where we'll begin, and we'll end by exploring how you can design your own larger patterns by combining different elements onto graph paper. In between, I'll aim to answer many of the questions most frequently asked.

WORKING FROM CHARTS

Until the pioneering work of the Kogin Lab, which began creating paper charts of traditional designs in the mid 20th century (see Introduction), traditional kogin patterns were passed on from stitcher to stitcher, with new pattern combinations being invented along the way. The earliest kogin books, including those published by Kogin Lab, feature many patterns shown only as stitched samples. Today, however, graph paper charts are universally used.

There are two main ways to create a kogin chart on graph paper: either each graph square represents one crossover point in the woven fabric, very much in the style of a cross stitch chart; or the graph lines themselves represent the threads. The first method is more regularly seen in the kogin pattern books published in the 1950s and 60s, where often just half the square is coloured in vertically, but the latter method, where graph lines represent the fabric weave, is more commonly used today.

The pattern charts in the Pattern Library use one graph line to represent one woven thread. The 'stitches' are shown by horizontal lines across one, two, three or more 'woven threads'. It is like looking at a drawing of the actual stitching and, therefore, easier to follow.

TIP

If you are stitching a pattern from a photograph of an antique kogin piece without a lot of detail, it is helpful to remember how the kogin and Nanbu hishizashi patterns work, mainly over odd and even numbers of threads respectively. As many charts in the Pattern Library are drawn from original pieces of kogin, you can also use these to help you work out the detail.

Kogin chart pattern style used from the 1950s onwards.

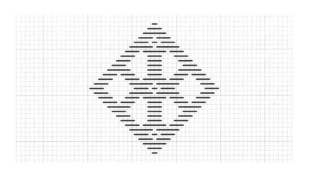

Modern kogin chart pattern as used in this book.

PREPARING THREAD AND FABRIC

Preparing a tied skein

Unlike stranded cotton (floss), soft cotton and tapestry wool, all of which are supplied in a 'pull skein', kogin thread is supplied in a tied skein, as are sashiko thread, cotton perle and hand-dyed yarns. To prepare kogin thread and other tied skein threads for use, slide off the skein band (if there is one). You will find the skein is tied together at one point; snip off the knot and cut through all the threads at that point. Slide the skein band back onto the threads (so you will know the brand and shade number if you need to reorder) and loosely plait. Draw out individual threads from the top of the plait as you need to use them.

Preparing fabric edges

Kogin fabric frays a lot, so oversew or zigzag stitch the raw edges before you begin stitching - this is especially important for large designs that will be well-handled as you work. Ideally use a machine-sewn zigzag on the widest setting, around ⅛in (3mm) long; if oversewing by hand, make sure your stitches stay within the seam allowance area, i.e. less than ⅜in (1cm) from the edge.

Finding the centre of the fabric

If stitching a motif centred on your fabric, find the centre of the fabric by folding it into quarters and creasing it firmly. Some projects require a final fold, to create eighths.

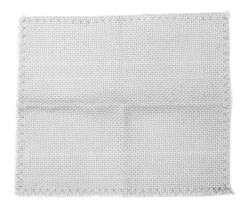

How long should my thread be?

The simple answer is as long as possible, as this requires fewer starts and stops, so saving time and using up less thread. If you opened your skein as shown in Preparing Thread and Fabric, the longest strand will be approx. 39in (1m), depending on thread brand and skein size.

To stitch a motif, you will start with the *maetate* (the row of stitches at the motif centre): use a whole length of thread as it comes off the skein plait (just over 1 yd/m). For continuous patterns or where the overall design requires you to start at the point of the motif, use half a thread length (approx. 18in/50cm).

If working with a softer thread more prone to fluffing up while stitching, such as soft cotton, knitting or tapestry wool, work with a shorter thread length (approx. 18in/50cm).

Multi-strand threads – kogin thread, stranded cotton (floss), 4-ply variegated cotton – may start to bunch up along the length as you stitch. If this happens, slide your needle right down the thread to the fabric and smooth the strands back together before resuming stitching.

To thread your needle, slightly flatten one end of the thread to help it go through the needle's eye. Alternatively, fold the thread over the eye of the needle to flatten it slightly and push it through. If the thread really will not go through the needle's eye, you may need a larger needle.

Where do I start?

Individual motifs centred on a piece of fabric will start with the *maetate* (foundation row) through the middle of the pattern. This is also best where one pattern nestles into a sideways V-shape created by two others, such as building up the motifs in the wall hanging project (see Projects: Wall Hanging).

If a pattern links to the top or bottom of another one, as seen on the cushion cover project (see Projects: Cushion Cover), start the next pattern at the top or bottom point, linking to the previous pattern, rather than across the *maetate* line. Leave a 'tail' around 2½–3in (6.4–7.6cm) long, which will be finished off by stitching into the back of the fabric when the pattern is complete (see Finishing Off).

maetate (foundation row)

The neko no ashi *(cat's paw) pattern.*

STITCHING KOGIN

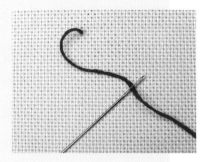

1. Start stitching at the centre with the *maetate* (foundation row). Depending on the pattern, the exact centre of the foundation row may be a stitch or a gap. If it is a single stitch, as for the *neko no ashi* (cat's paw) pattern shown in Where Do I Start?, start a couple of stitches to one side of the centre and sew the single stitch later (see step 5). Come up from the back of your fabric and give your thread a counterclockwise twist if necessary (see Preparing Thread and Fabric).

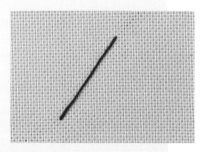

2. Pull half the thread through to start stitching. (You will use the second half to complete the rest of the row followed by the first half of the motif and it may be 'parked' out of the way temporarily by making a single random long stitch out to the corner of your fabric, so it doesn't get tangled up with the stitches – the photo shows the back of the fabric with this stitch.)

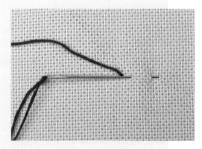

3. Following the pattern chart, stitch to one end of the row. Several stitches can be placed on the needle before pulling through in a 'sewing' motion, similar to sashiko stitching: the fabric is pleated onto the needle tip, gathered up slightly and eased out flat. Make sure your thread is not twisting and that the stitches are not pulled too tight.

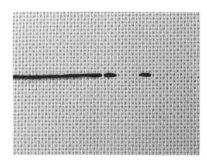

4. Unthread your needle and rethread it with the other end of your thread (the one 'parked' on the back in step 2). Following the pattern, bring this thread through to the front, ready to start sewing the other half of the *maetate* row. Keep your rows straight: take care not to skip over a horizontal thread and slip off the row you are stitching. Stitches should be slightly raised on the surface, not sinking into the fabric.

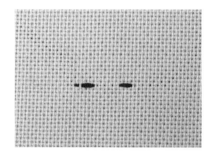

5. If you try to stitch over a single thread in one 'sewing' movement with a rocking action, like at the centre of this pattern, the short stitch will sink into the fabric and almost disappear. Work these as stab stitches, i.e. come up through the fabric and go back down again as two separate movements. Stitches over two threads can benefit from being worked this way too.

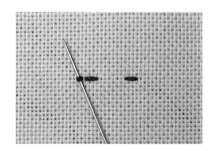

6. If a short stitch does disappear into the fabric, use your needle to raise up the stitch slightly before continuing with the stitching line, taking care not to split the thread.

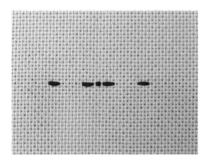

7. Stitch to the end of the *maetate* row. When the row is finished, check that your stitches are all going over and under the correct number of threads. You can now stitch the top half of the motif.

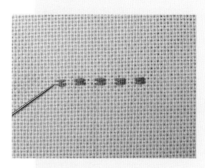

10. Some continuous patterns start the next row directly above the previous one. If the fabric's horizontal thread lies across the vertical one at this point, your last and first stitches will tend to slip back along the horizontal thread and slide under the vertical one, as indicated by the needle's point...

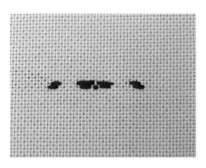

8. Turn and stitch the next whole row of the pattern. Most kogin motifs step diagonally over one thread at the end of the row, while Nanbu hishizashi patterns step over two, so there will be a short diagonal 'stitch' on the back between the row ends. Keep this as a small loop.

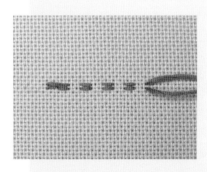

11. ... so work either the first or last stitch as a backstitch, to stop the stitches slipping under the vertical thread. Take care that the backstitch (the longer stitch on the reverse) is not too tight. The photo shows the backstitch on the reverse of the fabric.

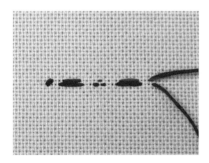

9. This small loop should be about ⅛in (3mm) maximum, so your stitching doesn't pull in and distort the fabric (the photo shows the back of the fabric). Continue following the chart to stitch the top half of the motif, then use the other end of the thread that was 'parked' in step 2 to stitch the bottom half.

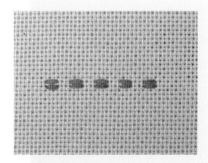

12. When this second row is complete, the backstitch will be indistinguishable from the running stitch on the right side.

How do I correct mistakes?

Everyone makes thread counting mistakes in kogin! So long as you take care unpicking your mistakes, you can quickly resolve any miscounting issues. Most often you will spot your mistake in the next row, as the pattern will not align as expected, so there usually isn't a lot to unpick. Unthread the needle and slide the tip under the last stitch, raise it up and pull it out. Unpick stitches one or two at a time (avoid individually pulling up stitches made over single threads as, because they are so small, it is easy to accidentally split the thread). Repeat until you are back to the mistake, rethread the needle and correct it. We all become experts at this 'unstitching' quite soon. If your thread becomes worn from too much unpicking, discard it and use a fresh thread.

Occasionally, you may not spot a mistake until later, when it may be easier to 'fudge' the rest of the pattern to fit rather than unpick a large section. If you didn't notice it, it is likely no one else will either.

Sometimes patterns have sections that look the same but are subtly changed, such as a variation in the number of rows on the centre side section of a frame lengthened or shortened to fit the centre motif (see pattern 214), or a different number of rows between a block of stitches (see pattern 216). Look out for these and make a note of any that appear in your chosen pattern.

FINISHING OFF

To finish the kogin, stitch the end of the thread in and out of the weave across the back of your work. To ensure the sewn-in thread ends are hidden, work single thread stitches as much as possible behind areas of the design that appear as longer stitches on the front of the panel. Be careful not to undo your final stitch as you begin, and stitch for 2-3in (5-7.6cm). There is no need to turn after several finishing stitches and stitch in the opposite direction, unless you have only a short area to finish off or on a point.

When completing a motif, you will be finishing on a point, so you will need to stitch back and forth two or three times on the back, instead of finishing off with a longer line, as shown right.

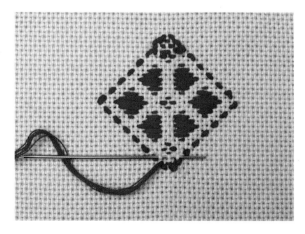

WORKING WITH
MULTIPLE COLOURS

You can use changes in thread colour to emphasise different stitch patterns in a kogin design, by contrasting frames and borders with motifs (see Projects: Table Runner), or by working a larger pattern with more subtle shade changes (see Projects: Mini Tote Bag). Stitching repeated columns or rows of motifs in different colours is also very effective (see Projects: Cushion Cover).

For multiple coloured frames, start with the central motif and stitch each subsequent border in a different colour.

Where motifs are arranged within a grid, begin with either a whole motif at the centre or a half motif at the top or bottom edge. The grid is stitched separately, in the second colour, growing it as you add motifs. By working this way, you are less liable to make mistakes counting the fabric threads than if you try to stitch an 'empty' grid and add the motifs later. *Do not* strand thread across the back of the grid anywhere that you plan to stitch a motif, as this will block off the back of the fabric with long float threads, preventing you from stitching other motifs later. If you add the motifs in vertical columns, it is possible to strand the thread across the back from the bottom of one motif to the top of the next, once the grid is stitched, without the need to start and finish each motif individually.

At the edge of a panel the thread can also 'travel' from one part of a design to another via single thread vertical stitches worked within the seam allowance, to be hidden once the kogin panel is made up into the finished project.

The back of pattern 109 from Motif Arrangements.

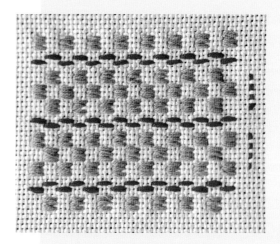

The dark pink thread travels down the side of the fabric from one section to the next in this combination of patterns 157 and 159 from Diagonal Borders and Frames.

DESIGNING KOGIN

If you would like to explore drawing up your own combinations of kogin patterns to make your finished projects unique, you'll need graph paper, pencils, an eraser and marker pens. I'd recommend using metric graph paper with lines every 2mm (12.5 squares to 1in/2.5cm), as the grid is large enough to see easily with sufficient space in between to be able to draw your 'stitch' lines accurately, but be aware your diagram will be around 50 per cent bigger than your finished stitching.

Working onto graph paper is ideal for designing larger kogin pieces, and by working in this way, kogin stitchers such as Setsu Maeda were able to develop larger, more complex panels (see Introduction: Kogin Revival). This is not as daunting as it may first seem as most kogin patterns are symmetrical vertically and horizontally, so it is only necessary to draw a quarter of the design, then 'flip' and repeat it. An exception to this rule is the *sayagata* (saya brocade) pattern, which has rotational rather than reflective symmetry.

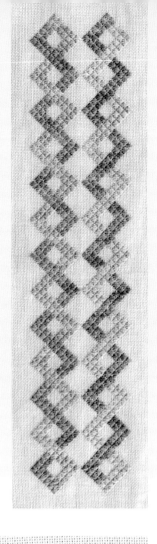

This spiral arrangement, stitched in hand dyed, six-strand embroidery cotton on linen, gives a simple kogin pattern a modern twist.

Sayagata kakomi (saya brocade enclosure) (see pattern 155), combined with simple diagonal borders.

Remember, for the charts in this book, the grid lines represent the woven threads of the fabric. The 'stitches' are drawn from the middle of one square to the middle of another across the grid 'thread' lines. If you draw the stitch lines in pencil first, you can erase mistakes as you work out your design, then ink them in with a bold marker pen so you can see them easily against the printed grid lines. Once you are fairly confident at drafting kogin patterns on paper, you can omit the pencil stage and go straight to a permanent marker, but it is a good idea to have some correction tape to hand to fix any small mistakes in your design. Larger drawing errors can be corrected by using repositionable sticky tape to attach a fresh section of graph paper over the problem area.

You can also combine kogin patterns directly onto your fabric, which is how the early kogin stitchers must have worked, but this can be a little hit and miss. Be prepared to unpick parts of the design that don't quite fit as expected (usually borders), or to 'fudge' the pattern to fit by stretching parts of the design or altering the corners - little adjustments like this are commonly seen on antique kogin jacket panels.

PATTERNS FROM OTHER SOURCES

The patterns in the Pattern Library are almost all traditional designs. If you start researching kogin patterns online or in modern Japanese books, you will find many designs that are original to those kogin authors, either variations on traditional patterns or that have been adapted from other pattern sources. For example, I have seen many kogin patterns that have been adapted from Norwegian smøyg embroidery, Scandinavian and Baltic embroidery designs, weaving patterns and Fair Isle knitting patterns. These will often be labelled 'kogin', and, while it is fun to incorporate these within kogin patterns, you should remain aware that these patterns did not originate in kogin or Nanbu hishizashi and will follow different conventions regarding stitch length combinations and other pattern elements.

Adjustments are often required as you stitch. For example, for this sampler I found that the outer royal blue border frame would not fit between the two turquoise borders. So, to avoid having to unpick it to move this frame pattern sideways by a stitch or two, I adapted it at the top and bottom points, which have a motif slightly separated out from the rest of the border.

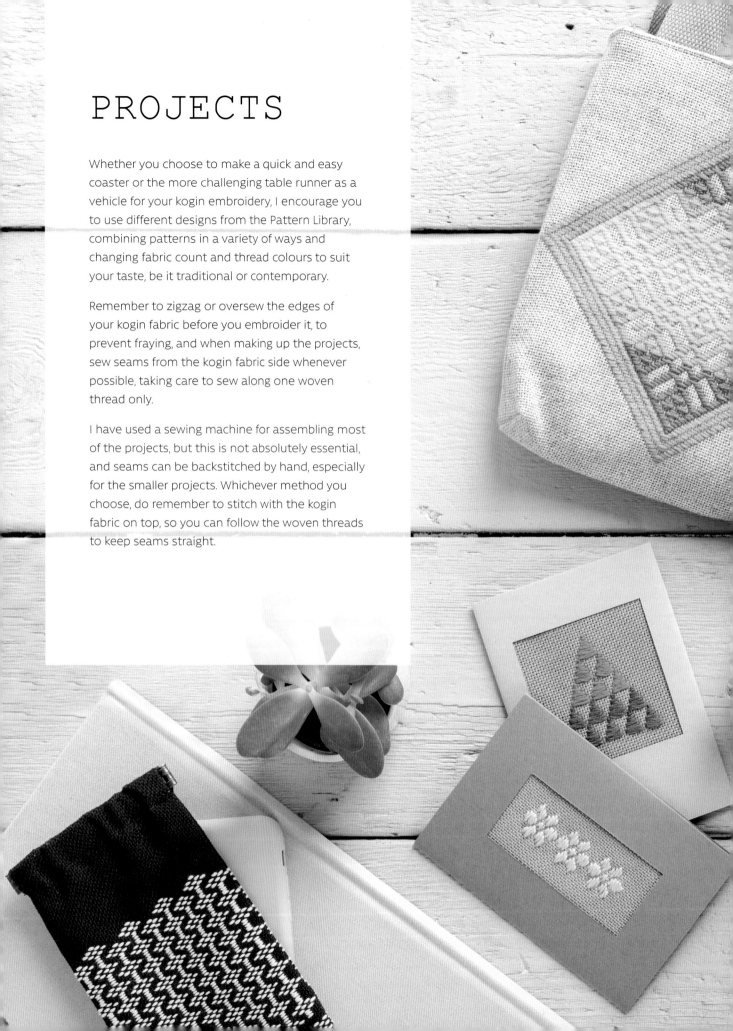

PROJECTS

Whether you choose to make a quick and easy coaster or the more challenging table runner as a vehicle for your kogin embroidery, I encourage you to use different designs from the Pattern Library, combining patterns in a variety of ways and changing fabric count and thread colours to suit your taste, be it traditional or contemporary.

Remember to zigzag or oversew the edges of your kogin fabric before you embroider it, to prevent fraying, and when making up the projects, sew seams from the kogin fabric side whenever possible, taking care to sew along one woven thread only.

I have used a sewing machine for assembling most of the projects, but this is not absolutely essential, and seams can be backstitched by hand, especially for the smaller projects. Whichever method you choose, do remember to stitch with the kogin fabric on top, so you can follow the woven threads to keep seams straight.

GREETINGS CARDS

Small kogin samples can be transformed into unique greetings cards suitable for any occasion using readily available aperture card blanks. When choosing your card, just make sure your kogin fabric adequately covers the aperture plus a little extra. A double-fold card gives the best finish as the extra fold neatly conceals the back of the embroidery, but if you only have a single-fold card, a piece of paper cut to size and secured in place with double-sided tape does the same job. Experiment with different thread and fabric colour combinations and have fun exploring.

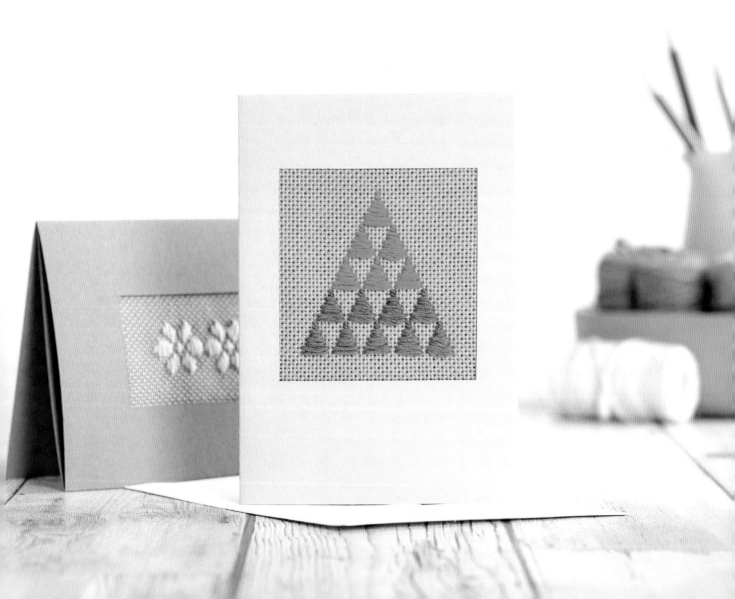

- Piece of kogin fabric (any thread count) at least ½in (1.3cm) larger than card aperture size all round
- Lightweight iron-on interfacing (optional), same size as kogin fabric*
- Kogin thread (exact quantity depends on kogin pattern selected)
- Card blank with aperture to fit your embroidery
- Masking tape
- Basic sewing kit (see Tools and Materials)

Backing the kogin with iron-on interfacing gives a nice solid finish.

FINISHED SIZE

Varies depending on the size of your card aperture

PATTERNS USED

(refer to Pattern Library)

Patterns 23 and 75

MAKING UP

1. Prepare and embroider the greetings card panel:
Oversew or zigzag the edges of the evenweave fabric (see Basic Techniques: Preparing Thread and Fabric). Select a design from the Pattern Library and begin stitching, referring to Basic Techniques: Stitching Kogin. (If you choose to stitch a continuous pattern rather than an individual or repeat motif, use the card aperture as a stencil to mark the design area onto your fabric using a water-soluble marker, then stitch approx. ⅛in (3mm) beyond the marked area.)

2. Finish the embroidered panel: Lightly press your finished kogin from the back. If you are using iron-on interfacing, cut a piece slightly smaller than the kogin fabric and attach it to the back of the embroidery following the manufacturer's instructions.

3. Make up the card: Open out the card blank, arrange the kogin behind the card aperture and use masking tape to hold the fabric in place. If you are using a double-fold card blank (see Fig 1), the extra fold will hide the back of the embroidery. If your card has a single fold as in Fig 2, use a piece of paper cut to fit the card panel and secure in place with strips of double-sided tape.

Fig 1

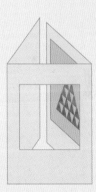

Fig 2

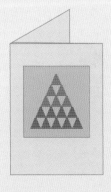

COASTER COLLECTION

This set of coasters is made from little squares of kogin worked on evenweave fabric of several different thread counts. To keep a coordinated look, choose a theme for your fabric and thread choices – mine were inspired by the autumn leaf colours of the Oirase Gorge in Aomori Prefecture, one of the most beautiful river valleys in Japan. If you want to avoid coasters with bulky corners, framing the kogin squares with strips of coordinating fabric is essential when using 18-count (or chunkier) weaves, but borders are optional if using finer weaves of 20-count or over.

▶ Fabric requirements for small bordered coaster

  » one 4in (10cm) square of evenweave fabric for embroidered panel

  » two 4 x 1½in (10 x 3.8cm) striped fabric strips for top and bottom borders

  » two 5½ x 1½in (14 x 3.8cm) striped fabric strips for side borders

  » one 5½in (14cm) plain cotton square for backing

▶ Fabric requirements for large bordered coaster

  » one 5in (12.7cm) square of evenweave fabric for embroidered panel

  » two 5 x 1½in (12.7 x 3.8cm) striped fabric strips for top and bottom borders

  » two 6½ x 1½in (16.5 x 3.8cm) striped fabric strips for side borders

  » one 6½in (16.5cm) plain cotton square for backing

▶ Fabric requirements for coaster without borders

  » one 5in (12.7cm) square of evenweave fabric for embroidered panel

  » one 5in (12.7cm) plain cotton square for backing

▶ Kogin or other six-strand embroidery threads (exact quantities depend on kogin patterns selected)

▶ Sewing thread to tone with fabrics

▶ Basic sewing kit (see Tools and Materials)

FINISHED SIZE

Small bordered coaster: 4¾in (12cm) square

Large bordered coaster: 5¾in (14.6cm) square

Coaster without borders: 4¼in (10.8cm) square

I stitched the large bordered yellow ochre and small bordered cherry red coaster with kogin thread on 18-count evenweave fabric. For the remaining three coasters I used variegated six-strand embroidery threads, working the embroidery for the small bordered red coaster and the russet coaster without borders on 20-count evenweave fabric, and the small bordered dark peach coaster on 21-count.

PATTERNS USED

(refer to Pattern Library)

Patterns 11, 21, 66, 100, 163, 193 and 194

MAKING UP

1. Prepare and embroider the kogin panels: Oversew or zigzag the edges of the evenweave fabric squares (see Basic Techniques: Preparing Thread and Fabric). Working on each prepared fabric square one at a time, select a design from the Pattern Library and begin stitching, referring to Basic Techniques: Stitching Kogin. When the embroidery is complete, lightly press your finished kogin from the back.

2. Attach the border strips to the bordered coasters: With right sides together and raw edges aligning, machine sew the two shorter border strips to the top and bottom of the kogin square using a ⅜in (1cm) seam allowance. Fold borders outwards and press. Sew the two longer border strips to each side of the kogin square in the same way.

3. Add the backing panels and finish: Place the matching backing fabric square to each coaster front panel, right sides together, and pin in place. Starting and finishing with a few backstitches, machine sew around the edges with a ⅜in (1cm) seam allowance, leaving a 2½–3in (6.4–7.6cm) gap on one side. Trim off corners to about ⅛in (3mm) from the stitch line. Bag out each coaster (i.e. turn it the right way out through the unsewn gap) and carefully push the corners out. Turn in the seam allowance at the gap and invisibly slipstitch to close. Press lightly.

PLACE MAT

A place mat is a quick and easy project to make, provided you restrict your kogin embroidery only to the areas that will be visible to the diner once the place mat is set! I was inspired to create the original tiny trees pattern in the bottom corners of my mat by a wall light sculpture that I had seen at Aomori Museum of Art. 'Aomori' means 'green forest', so I chose to stitch the pattern in three different shades of green, sloping with a slightly different step on each side to create the impression of trees on facing hillsides.

YOU WILL NEED

- 18-count evenweave fabric 13 x 18in (33 x 45.7cm) for front panel

- Striped fabric 13 x 20in (33 x 50.8cm) for backing*

- Kogin thread: four 39in (1m) lengths of two different shades of light green and two 39in (1m) lengths of darker green

- Sewing thread to tone with fabrics

- Basic sewing kit (see Tools and Materials)

*The striped backing fabric is larger than the front panel fabric as it is wrapped to the front at each side to create a self-bound border. To create a different look, you could use a small-scale printed cotton instead of a stripe.

FINISHED SIZE

12 x 17½in (30.5 x 44.5cm)

PATTERNS USED

(refer to Pattern Library)

Pattern 73

MAKING UP

1. **Prepare and embroider the front panel fabric:** Oversew or zigzag the edges of the evenweave fabric (see Basic Techniques: Preparing Thread and Fabric). Referring to Basic Techniques: Stitching Kogin, begin to stitch the bottom row of the kogin pattern, starting approximately 1in (2.5cm) in from the sides and bottom edge of the evenweave fabric. Follow the photograph of the finished embroidery and remember to change thread colours as you stitch the rows of trees, slanting the inner edge of the pattern as shown.

2. **Assemble the place mat:** Use a ⅜in (1cm) seam allowance throughout. Place the kogin panel and the backing fabric right sides together and pin at the sides only, lining up the raw edges: note that the backing is longer than the front panel. Machine sew together at the sides only, then press the seams towards the backing.

3. Now pin the top and bottom edges together, making sure that the front (kogin) panel is centred, so that the striped backing fabric will wrap evenly to the front of the place mat when finished. Starting and finishing with a few backstitches, machine sew along the top and bottom edges, leaving a gap approx. 4in (10cm) at the centre of the bottom edge. Trim off the corners within the seam allowance, but do not cut right up to the stitches – about half way is fine.

4. Bag out the place mat (i.e. turn it the right way out through the unsewn gap) and push the corners out. Turn in the seam allowance at the gap and invisibly slipstitch to close. Press lightly. The striped backing fabric now forms a narrow border at each side of the place mat; to hold it in place, hand sew small, neat running stitches approx. ⅛in (3mm) from each edge, stitching from the back through the backing and seam allowances only, taking a tiny running stitch on top then sliding a longer stitch approx. ⅛in (3mm) through the layers.

CUSHION COVER

Square cushions are an ideal format for kogin whether you choose a simple repeating design, like me, or an elaborate medallion motif. The *neko no ashi* (cat's paw) pattern that I have used is easy to stitch, but it can be swapped with another small motif if you prefer. The shaded autumnal colour scheme was suggested by a chance encounter of nine soft cotton skeins in a thread basket but can be easily adapted to a different inspiration. Finish the cushion with a quick and easy envelope back; match the front panel fabric, or choose a coordinating stripe for a more colourful effect.

- 18-count evenweave fabric 19in (48.3cm) square for cushion front

- Nine 11yd (10m) skeins of soft cotton or 19¾yd (18m) skeins of kogin thread* in colours of your choosing

- Two pieces of coordinating fabric 19 x 12in (48.3 x 30.5cm) for cushion back

- Sewing thread to tone with fabrics

- Basic sewing kit (see Tools and Materials)

- Cushion pad 18in (45cm)** square

*You may need more thread if you choose a slightly larger motif: this design used a whole 11yd (10m) skein of soft cotton thread per colour with very little left over, so be very economical with your thread if using these smaller skeins.

**The metric cushion pad is slightly smaller so the cushion cover will be a little looser; the cushion cover can be sewn with slightly wider seams in step 2 to achieve the same fit.

FINISHED SIZE

18in (45.7cm) square

PATTERNS USED

(refer to Pattern Library)

Pattern 17

MAKING UP

1. Prepare and embroider the front panel fabric:
Oversew or zigzag the edges of the evenweave fabric (see Basic Techniques: Preparing Thread and Fabric). Arrange the threads in your preferred order and make a note. Using the middle thread, start stitching the kogin at the centre of the fabric (see Basic Techniques: Stitching Kogin). Beginning with the central column of motifs, stitch each in turn, and finish one before starting the next. There is a space of three threads between each motif and each column, which can be reduced or increased if an alternative motif is used. Lightly press the finished kogin from the wrong side.

2. Make up the cushion cover: Stitch a neat ¼in (6mm) double hem on one long edge of each piece of backing fabric and zigzag the remaining raw edges. Place one of the backing pieces on top of the front panel, right sides together and raw edges aligned, and pin in place (Fig 1); then add the second backing piece (Fig 2). Machine sew around the edge with a ½in (1.3cm) seam allowance. Clip the corners and turn right side out. Insert a cushion pad through the gap.

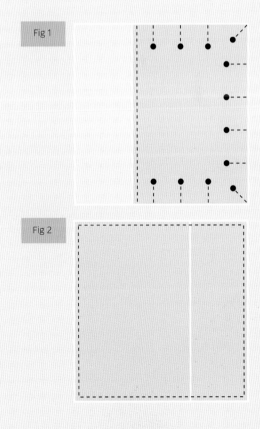

Fig 1

Fig 2

SMALL PURSES

Snap purse frames are very popular in Japan, and these small lined purses are a very cute way of displaying your kogin embroidery – they may be a little fiddly to make but they're worth it. Try to choose a lining fabric to coordinate with the colour scheme of the outer purse – for example, on the little russet purse I used blue batik to complement the kogin thread shade used. Purse frames often come with a pattern that you can use for the shape of your purse; if so you can go straight to step 2, but if not my instructions show how to draw your own.

YOU WILL NEED

▶ Two pieces of evenweave fabric slightly larger than the purse pattern for purse front and back*

▶ Two pieces of patchwork cotton slightly larger than the purse pattern for lining

▶ Two pieces of lightweight iron-on interfacing slightly larger than the purse pattern (optional)

▶ Kogin threads (exact quantities depend on kogin patterns selected)

▶ One metal purse frame per purse, crimp or stitch style, approx. 3⅛in (8cm) wide*

▶ Thin card for making purse pattern if required

▶ Polycotton thread to tone with fabrics

▶ For crimp frames only: fine paper packing string, impact adhesive, toothpick, awl, purse clasp pliers

▶ For stitch frames only: coordinating jeans thread or no.12 sewing thread

▶ Basic sewing kit (see Tools and Materials)

*If using an 18-count evenweave fabric, a stitch purse frame is best as it would be a tight fit for a crimp frame; either a stitch or crimp style frame is fine for 20-count and finer weaves as they are easier to assemble.

FINISHED SIZE

4 x 3½in (10 x 9cm) although this may vary depending on the size of your purse frame

PATTERNS USED

(refer to Pattern Library)

Patterns 3, 6, 19 and 39

MAKING UP

1. **Make the purse pattern:** One half is drawn first then the template is folded to cut out, to make a symmetrical pattern. Draw a vertical line in the centre of a piece of thin card (Fig 1a). Fully open the purse frame and place it on the card so that the snap fastener aligns with the vertical line you have drawn. Draw around the top of the frame to its shoulder (where the curve slightly changes shape) and mark a short line at right angles to the frame edge (Fig 1b). Pivot the frame at the shoulder point and continue the drawn line down to the hinge (Fig 1c). Draw a horizontal line linking the hinge point to the vertical line, then draw the shape of the purse below the hinge point (Fig 1d), making it rounded, squarer or even slightly pointed as you wish. Draw a ⅜in (1cm) seam allowance line around the bottom of the purse only, from the hinge point to the vertical centre line (Fig 1e). Fold the card in half along the vertical line and cut out the marked shape through both layers to make a symmetrical pattern (Fig 1f).

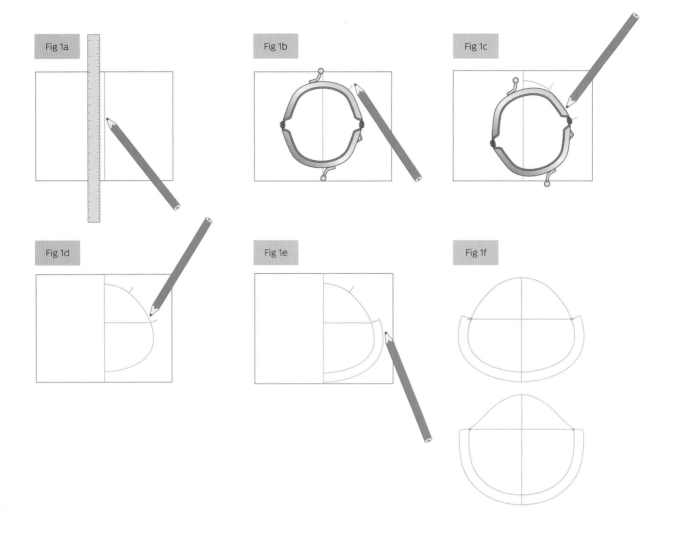

| Fig 1a | Fig 1b | Fig 1c |
| Fig 1d | Fig 1e | Fig 1f |

2. **Prepare and embroider the kogin fabric:** Oversew or zigzag the edges of the evenweave fabric pieces (see Basic Techniques: Preparing Thread and Fabric). Use your purse pattern to mark the purse shape onto each piece, but do not cut out at this stage. Using the drawn purse shape as a guide to your stitching area, choose a kogin pattern to stitch. Note: if using a continuous pattern, do not stitch within the seam allowance in the bottom half of the purse, and to ensure that the stitched panel does not become too thick to fit into the purse frame, do not stitch up to the top of the panel - a rule that should also be applied when stitching individual motifs. Referring to Basic Techniques: Stitching Kogin, stitch your chosen motifs.

3. **Finish the embroidered panels:** Press the kogin lightly from the back. If using iron-on interfacing, attach it to the back of each panel following the manufacturer's instructions. Machine stitch a line of stay stitching along the top edge of each purse shape, from hinge point to hinge point, a generous ¹⁄₁₆in (1.5mm) from the edge - this will help to prevent fraying and stretching. Cut out the purse panels along the marked lines.

4. **Sew the purse panels together:** Pin the purse panels right sides together and machine stitch along the seam allowance at the bottom half of the purse, starting and finishing with a few backstitches. Clip the seam allowance and finger press open, then turn the purse right side out.

5. **Cut and attach the lining:** Use the purse pattern to cut out two lining pieces from the patchwork cotton, and sew together as in step 4, clipping seams and finger pressing seams open, but *do not* turn through to the right side. Place the lining inside the purse and use a hand sewn running stitch, with an occasional backstitch, to join the lining to the purse around the top edges, working on top of the line of machine sewn stay stitching. To continue, follow the instructions for steps 6 and 7 for the crimp frame, or step 8 for the stitch frame purse depending on which type of frame you have.

MAKING UP THE CRIMP FRAME PURSE

6 . **Assemble the crimp frame purse:** Note: my instruction may differ from the frame manufacturer's assembly advice as I have found that, to accommodate the thickness of the kogin fabric, it is easier to blanket stitch the paper packing string supplied to the top edge of the purse before crimping the frame in place. Cut two pieces of the paper packing string slightly shorter than the curve of the frame. Take one piece and centre it on the inside top edge of one side of the purse. Working from one end of the string to the other, stitch it in place with small blanket stitches between the machine stay stitching and the edge of the lining fabric, making sure to keep it centred as you sew. Continue the blanket stitch around the hinge area, then repeat to stitch the second piece of paper packing string along the other side (Fig 2).

7 . With the purse frame opened flat, use the toothpick to apply a small amount of impact adhesive inside the groove of one side of the frame. Working from the inside of the purse and starting at the centre of the frame outwards, use the awl to push the top edge of one side of the purse into the glued side of the frame. It is a little fiddly to do, but persevere. Be sure to push the paper-string edge right up into the groove of the metal frame (a small flat screwdriver or the back edge of an unpicker can be useful to tuck in any stray fabric threads). Repeat to secure the top edge of the other side of the purse into the frame, then take the pliers and crimp the purse frame down onto the fabric, just above the hinges on each side, using a small piece of scrap fabric inside the pliers' jaws to avoid scratching the metal purse frame (Fig 3).

MAKING UP THE STITCH FRAME PURSE

8 . **Assemble the stitch frame purse:** With the purse frame opened flat and working one side at a time, insert the top edge of the purse into the groove of the frame and centre it. Use scrap thread to temporarily stitch the fabric in place at the centre and either end of the frame, just above the hinges (shown in white in Fig 4). Working from the right side of the purse and starting in the centre of the frame just below the clasp, use jeans thread or no.12 sewing thread to stitch the fabric into the frame with running stitch (shown in red in Fig 4). (It is easier to hide the thread ends if you start here and leave a 'tail' of thread that you can knot together with the working thread at the end, before sewing both ends in just under the frame.) Once the first line of running stitch is complete, stitch in the opposite direction sewing alternately to the first row, so the gaps between the first line of running stitches are filled by the second row of running stitches.

Fig 2

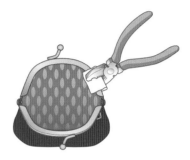

Fig 3

Fig 4

MINI TOTE BAG

The front of a simple mini tote bag is a great place to stitch this large kogin panel, which combines several motifs and a border frame. Inspired by a design found on an antique Nishi kogin kimono stitched in white on deep indigo, my colourful modern interpretation uses shades of yellow ochre to create an ombre effect. Only small amounts of each colour are required for the central motif, making it an ideal project for using up thread remnants, while the mid value shade chosen for the border frame coordinates beautifully with the bag lining and handles.

YOU WILL NEED

▶ 18-count evenweave fabric 18½ x 9in (47 x 23cm) for bag outer

▶ Five or six kogin thread colours, shading from light to dark, 2⅛–6½yd (2–6m) of each*

▶ Coordinating lightweight cotton 18½ x 9in (47 x 23cm) for bag lining

▶ Two 13in (33cm) lengths of 1in (2.5cm) wide cotton webbing for bag handles

▶ Sewing thread to tone with fabrics

▶ Basic sewing kit (see Tools and Materials)

*6½yd (6m) is the amount required for the mid value (medium golden yellow) shade used in the central motif and border frame; all other threads are used in smaller quantities.

FINISHED SIZE

8¾ x 7½in (22.2 x 19cm) excluding handles

PATTERNS USED

(refer to Pattern Library)

Pattern 228

MAKING UP

1. **Prepare and embroider the bag panel fabric:**
Oversew or zigzag the edges of the evenweave fabric (see Basic Techniques: Preparing Thread and Fabric). Arrange the threads in your preferred order and make a note. Fold the fabric in half and lightly press to mark the baseline of the bag. Find the centre of the front side of the bag by folding in half one way and then the other, and start stitching the kogin, following the centre line in the pattern chart and referring to Basic Techniques: Stitching Kogin. Use the lightest thread for the centre, shading through the other threads equally on either side. Once the central motif is complete, stitch the triple border frame.

2. **Make the bag outer and lining:** With the kogin bag panel folded right sides together and using a ⅜in (1cm) seam allowance, machine sew down each side to make the bag outer, starting and finishing all construction seams with a few backstitches. Use the lining fabric to make the bag lining in the same way but leave a 4in (10cm) gap unsewn in the second side for turning the bag right side out in step 5. Press open the seams on both bag outer and lining. If you prefer a flatter bag (suitable for an e-reader or mini tablet), omit step 3.

3. **Shape the base of the bag:** Keeping both bag outer and lining inside out, fold the bottom corners on each to make a point (see Fig 1). Mark a line at right angles to the seam, ¾in (1.9cm) from the point, then pin and machine sew across to create a triangular flap of fabric. To reduce bulk, cut off the flaps from the corners of the lining only to about ⅜in (1cm) from the stitch line. (*Do not* trim the corners of the bag outer as the kogin fabric frays easily.)

4. **Attach the handles:** Turn the bag outer right side out. Place the webbing strips on the right side of the bag outer front and back, so that the ends of the webbing overlap the top edge by ½in (1.3cm) and with a 3in (7.6cm) gap in between (see Fig 2). Make sure that the webbing handles are not twisted and then tack (baste) in place.

> TIP
>
> Alternatively, make simple
> handles from coordinating
> material. Cut two pieces
> 13 x 4in (33 x 10cm) along
> the fabric grain and follow
> the instructions for making
> hanging tabs (see Projects:
> Wall Hanging).

5. **Join the bag outer and lining:** Keeping the lining turned inside out and the bag outer right side out, place the bag outer inside the lining, taking care to line up the top edge and the side seams. Machine sew around the top of the bag, sewing the lining to the bag outer with a ⅜in (1cm) seam allowance. Turn the bag right side out through the unsewn gap in the lining side seam. Press the seam at the top of the bag. Machine or hand sew around the top of the bag, about ⅛in (3mm) from the edge. Turn the bag inside out and slipstitch the gap in the lining closed.

Fig 1

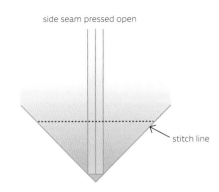

side seam pressed open

stitch line

Fig 2

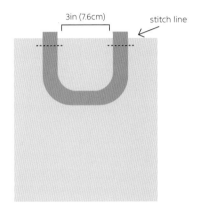

3in (7.6cm)

stitch line

WALL HANGING

Many of the basic on-point motifs of kogin, known as *modoko*, have been combined in this contemporary wall hanging, sampling many different designs. I started in the centre of my fabric with the *yokko gori* (group of four) motif stitched with a pink-red thread, and the sampler grew organically from there. Patterns were added one after another, stitched with oddments of purple, lilac and pink thread, with the point of one design nestling into the corners of others. The finished panel is edged with an easy mitre-effect border made from striped *tsumugi* (Japanese slubbed cotton) and backed with a coordinating fabric.

▶ 18-count evenweave fabric 28 x 14in (71.1 x 35.6cm) for sampler panel

▶ About a dozen kogin thread colours of your choosing*

▶ Striped fabric for border and hanging loops:
  » two 33½ x 3½in (85 x 9cm) strips for side borders
  » two 19½ x 3½in (49.5 x 9cm) strips for top and bottom borders
  » five 3½ x 4in (9 x 10cm) strips for hanging loops

▶ Coordinating fabric 33½ x 19½in (85 x 49.5cm) for backing

▶ Sewing thread to tone with fabrics

▶ Basic sewing kit (see Tools and Materials)

*The exact amount of thread needed will vary depending on how many motifs you decide to stitch: the total amount for the sampler wall hanging as shown is equivalent to approximately six 19¾yd (18m) skeins.

FINISHED SIZE

32¾ x 18¾in (83.2 x 47.6cm) with border

PATTERNS USED

Most of the patterns in the Motifs section of the Pattern Library were used to make this sampler. For a full list of the patterns used refer to the Pattern Identifier photograph.

MAKING UP

1. Prepare and embroider the centre panel fabric:
Oversew or zigzag the edges of the evenweave fabric (see Basic Techniques: Preparing Thread and Fabric), then find the centre by folding it in half one way and then the other. Start stitching the kogin at the centre of the fabric beginning with pattern 19, referring to the Pattern Identifier photograph and Basic Techniques: Stitching Kogin. Sew a second motif lining up with one edge of the first motif, and then add more motifs, continuing to refer to the Pattern Identifier photograph as you do so. There is a space of one thread between adjacent motifs, but this can be increased if you wish. If a motif is lined up with the corner of an adjacent motif, it will be easier to start stitching at the point, rather than in the centre line of the motif. However, where a motif nestles into a V-shaped corner, begin stitching it in the centre line. Lightly press finished kogin from the wrong side.

TIP

Use darker or brighter threads for smaller motifs and those towards the middle of the design.

2 . Add side borders to sampler panel: With right sides together, place the 33½ x 3½in (85 x 9cm) border strips, one on each side of the sampler panel, so that the edges are aligned and there is an even 2¾in (7cm) overlap at top and bottom (Fig 1); pin in place. (If you are using an ombre or striped fabric, take care to arrange the strips so the stripes mirror each other.) Machine sew each border strip to the sampler panel using a ⅜in (1cm) seam allowance. Fold side borders outwards and press seams (Fig 2).

3 . Add top and bottom borders to sampler panel: Take the 19½ x 3½in (49.5 x 9cm) top and bottom border strips and fold the ends of each to form a triangle on the reverse of the fabric (see Fig 3), taking care to match up stripes or ombre shading with the side borders. With right sides together, place one strip to align with the top edge of the sampler panel (see Fig 4), and pin. Note that the ends of the mitres will match up with the side panels ⅜in (1cm) from the edge rather than right at the fabric edge (see Fig 5 for detail), and this marks where the stitching line will be (see white dashed line on Figs 4 and 5). Machine sew the top border strip to the sampler panel using a ⅜in (1cm) seam allowance. Sew the remaining border strip to the bottom of the sampler panel. Fold top and bottom borders outwards and press seams (Fig 6). Hand sew the mitre fold to the side border at each corner, then trim away the excess fabric on the reverse to leave a ⅜in (1cm) seam allowance.

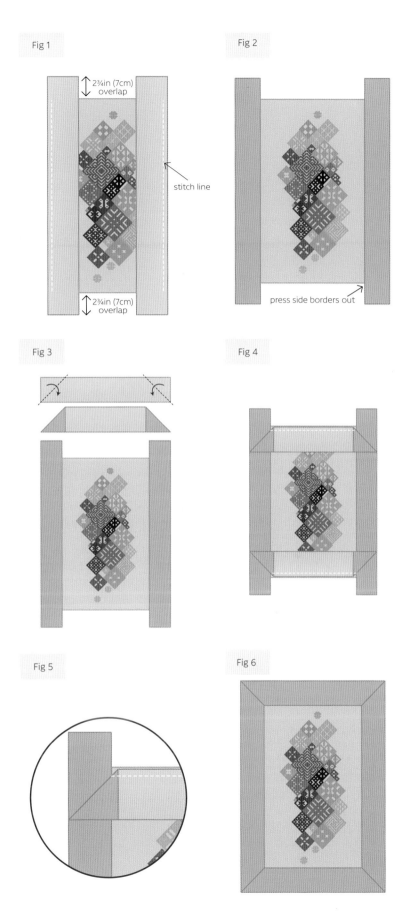

Fig 1

2¾in (7cm) overlap

stitch line

2¾in (7cm) overlap

Fig 2

press side borders out

Fig 3

Fig 4

Fig 5

Fig 6

Pattern Identifier

Refer to Pattern Library: Motifs for details of stitching the patterns. The motifs are mostly spaced just one thread apart, although occasionally there is a slightly wider gap to allow for the different motif sizes.

4 . Make and position the hanging loops: Take each of the 3½ x 4in (9 x 10cm) strips and fold, press and stitch following Fig 7 to make finished strips measuring ¾ x 4in (1.9 x 10cm). Fold each prepared strip in half to make five hanging loops. Pin one loop at each end of the top edge of the sampler front panel with raw edges aligned (see Fig 8), positioning them ⅝in (1.7cm) from the side edge. Fold the sampler front panel in half to find the centre of the top edge and pin a loop in place there, then pin the remaining loops half way between the centre loop and the side loops. Tack (baste) the loops in place.

5 . Add the backing and finish: Place the sampler front panel and backing fabric right sides together and pin around the edge. Machine sew with a ⅜in (1cm) seam allowance, leaving a 6in (15cm) gap at the centre of the bottom edge. Trim off the corners within the seam allowance, but do not cut right up to the stitches – about half way is fine. Bag out the hanging (i.e. turn it the right way out through the unsewn gap) and ease the corners out so they are nice and sharp. Lay it flat and smooth it out. Turn in the seam allowances at the gap, pin or tack (baste) and slipstitch closed. To keep the backing in place, working from the back and using small, neat hand stitches, sew all the way around the hanging ¼in (6mm) from the edge through the backing and seam allowance only.

Fig 7

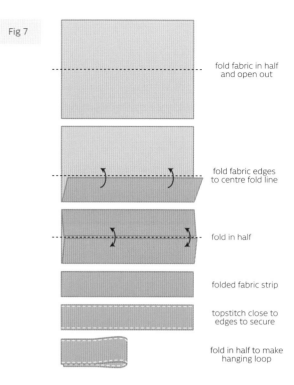

fold fabric in half and open out

fold fabric edges to centre fold line

fold in half

folded fabric strip

topstitch close to edges to secure

fold in half to make hanging loop

Fig 8

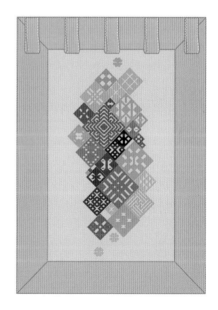

TABLE RUNNER

A large project such as a table runner gives the space needed to explore a more complex kogin pattern, and this one was based on a Higashi kogin jacket from Tokyo's Japan Folk Crafts Museum. This pattern combines kogin motifs with a zigzag border in variegated thread, both worked over an odd number of threads, with an outer border more akin to Nanbu hishizashi design (also in variegated thread) stitched over an even number of threads. Of course, any long, narrow kogin design would work. The runner is backed with a coordinating fabric and finished with a drawn threadwork hemstitch fringe at each end.

*The front panel was cut across the full width of the kogin fabric; if making a longer table runner, cut the panel parallel to the selvedge.

**I chose a plain cotton in a coordinating shade to match the yellow ochre evenweave fabric.

***The four-strand variegated cotton thread was used whole for the side section embroidery and split to use just two strands for the drawn thread hemstitch fringe border.

FINISHED SIZE

12 x 33in (30.5 x 84cm)

PATTERNS USED

(refer to Pattern Library)

Pattern 231

MAKING UP

1. Prepare the front panel fabric: Oversew or zigzag the edges of the evenweave fabric (see Basic Techniques: Preparing Thread and Fabric), then find the centre by folding it in half one way and then the other.

2. Stitch the central motifs: I used an ice-blue kogin thread to stitch the on-point pattern that runs down the middle of the runner. There are seven whole motifs and two half motifs with twelve fabric threads in between each, and the stitches are worked over an *odd* number of threads. Referring to Basic Techniques: Stitching Kogin, stitch the motif at the centre of the runner, starting with the *maetate* (foundation row) through the middle of the motif. Then, working outwards from the centre motif, stitch subsequent motifs, taking care to count the twelve threads in between motifs, from one point to another.

3 . Stitch the side sections: I used a variegated thread to stitch the sections that run down the side of the central on-point pattern, which consists of a zigzag pattern that frames the on-point motif and a dots/hexagon border, and each side of the runner is worked separately with the zigzag stitches over three threads and the dots/hexagons over varying even numbers of thread. Starting at the centre of the runner, begin stitching at the zigzag point towards the dots/hexagon border, working each row of the side section pattern continuously. For the pattern of repeated rows of little dots, make the turn to the next row at the outside edge with the last stitch of one pair of stitches (which forms one 'dot') with the first of the next pair of 'dot' stitches, to avoid the final stitch slipping along the weave (refer to Basic Techniques: Stitching Kogin, steps 10–12 for more information). Continue to stitch the side section pattern, working towards the ends of the runner. When all the embroidery has been completed, press the kogin lightly from the back.

4 . Work drawn threadwork hemstitch fringe border:
Starting with the fifth thread after the end of the kogin stitches at each end of the table runner panel, carefully remove five or six threads from the weave running across the panel (see Fig 1a). Working across each end of the panel in turn and following Fig 1b, use two strands of varigated cotton to stitch the hemstitch, beginning and ending ½in (1.3cm) from the sides.

5 . Carefully unravel the threads ½in (1.3cm) from the sides at each short end of the embroidered panel and darn through alternate threads back into the seam allowance (Fig 2).

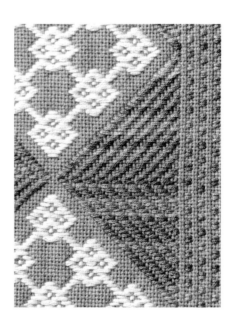

Fig 1a
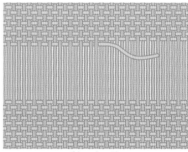
fringe length

Fig 1b
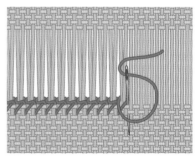
remove threads after hemstitching is complete

Fig 2
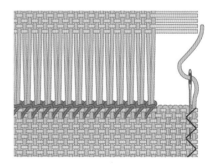

TIP

Darning the threads neatens the ends of the fabric threads and the darned area will disappear into the side seams once the backing is added.

6 . Add backing and finish: Fold under and press a generous hem allowance at each short end of the backing fabric, so that the folded edge will sit just behind the straight stitches of the hemstitch line at either end of the runner. Pin the kogin and backing fabric right sides together and machine sew along each long side with a ½in (1.3cm) seam allowance, starting and finishing with a few backstitches. Turn the runner through to the right side and press. Hold the side seams in place with small, neat hand stitches sewn from the reverse through the backing and seam allowances only. Finish by hand sewing the folded hem of the backing in place at each end of the runner, just behind the hemstitch. Trim off the last thread from the fabric selvedge and unravel the remaining threads to make the fringe.

DRAWSTRING BAGS

Always useful to store small items such as sewing equipment, these drawstring bags known as *kinchaku* are traditionally used as kimono accessories. The blue bag is stitched on 18-count evenweave with a traditional motif centred at the base of the bag, accented with an extra border in taupe kogin thread. The second bag has several Nanbu hishizashi patterns stitched in soft cotton on natural 20-count linen and is slightly longer to allow space for the patterns. The drawstring section at the top of each bag is made from more finely woven coordinating fabrics so they'll gather up easily, and the ends of the drawstring are finished with pretty flower trims.

YOU WILL NEED FOR BLUE BAG

▶ One piece of 18-count evenweave fabric 13 x 9in (33 x 23cm) for bag body

▶ Blue cotton patchwork fabric or similar
  » two 3 x 9in (7.6 x 23cm) pieces for bag top
  » one 17½ x 9in (44.5 x 23cm) piece for lining
  » two 3½in (9cm) squares for flower trims

▶ Two 20in (50.8cm) lengths of cord for drawstring

▶ Two 19¾yd (18m) skeins of kogin thread: one white and one taupe

▶ Sewing thread to tone with fabrics

▶ Basic sewing kit (see Tools and Materials)

YOU WILL NEED FOR LINEN BAG

▶ One piece of 20-count evenweave linen fabric 13½ x 9in (34.3 x 23cm) for bag body

▶ Fine natural linen patchwork fabric or similar
  » two 3 x 9in (7.6 x 23cm) pieces for bag top
  » one 18 x 9in (45.7 x 23cm) piece for lining
  » two 3½in (9cm) squares for flower trims

▶ Two 20in (50.8cm) lengths of cord for drawstring

▶ Seven 11yd (10m) skeins of soft cotton thread: two aubergine purple, two chartreuse yellow, one light grey, one dark grey and one yellow ochre

▶ Sewing thread to tone with fabrics

▶ Basic sewing kit (see Tools and Materials)

FINISHED SIZE

Blue bag: 8⅜ x 7½in (21 x 19cm)

Linen bag: 8⅞ x 7½in (22.4 x 19cm)

PATTERNS USED

(refer to Pattern Library)

Blue bag: Patterns 44, 162 and 163

Linen bag: Patterns 193, 203, 210 and 221

MAKING UP

1. Prepare and embroider the blue bag body:
Oversew or zigzag the edges of the evenweave fabric (see Basic Techniques: Preparing Thread and Fabric), then find the centre by folding it in half one way and then the other. Working from the centre line outwards and referring to Basic Techniques: Stitching Kogin, stitch the large kogin motif using white thread and referring to Fig 1.

Fig 1

2. Add the taupe border, starting at the side point of the completed centre motif. Note that the vertical spacing in the taupe border is slightly adjusted to fit the centre motif, so there are stacks of eight horizontal stitches in each long diagonal section, but only seven in the long diagonal section at the centre of each quarter of the pattern.

3. Now add the white border, starting at the top centre point of the taupe and stitching down either side, then turn the embroidery to complete the border, again starting at the top centre point and stitching down each side. Note that as this border does not meet itself at the sides of the bag, there is no need to adjust the pattern.

4. Prepare and embroider the linen bag body: Oversew or zigzag the edges of the evenweave fabric (see Basic Techniques: Preparing Thread and Fabric), then find the centre by folding it in half one way and then the other. Follow Fig 2 and work the central motif – pattern 221 – using aubergine thread, referring to Basic Techniques: Stitching Kogin and starting the stitching at the centre line. Continue adding pattern 221 motifs to the top and bottom of the first motif, starting at the point of each stitched motif, to complete the central column of nine aubergine motifs. There is no need to start and finish the thread with each individual motif – you can continue the thread from one motif to the next.

5. Stitch each column of chartreuse yellow motifs – pattern 203 – individually, starting at each end of the bag with the point of the end motif.

6. Stitch the two columns of grey motifs – pattern 210 – as individual motifs, alternating the thread colours and starting and finishing with each motif.

7. Finish the sides of the embroidered panel with pattern 193 worked with yellow ochre thread. You can 'travel' the thread from one pattern to the next by taking several single thread stitches vertically in the side seam area.

Fig 2

TIP

The bag assembly instructions are the same for both bags. Use ⅜in (1cm) seam allowances unless specifically instructed otherwise, and start and finish all seams with a few backstitches each time.

8. **Assemble the bag body:** Machine sew the bag top pieces to either end of the embroidered bag body panel and press the seams towards the bag top pieces. Fold the panel in half with right sides together and bag top pieces aligned, and pin in place. Starting from the bag top, machine sew the first 1in (2.5cm) section at either side, then leave a 1in (2.5cm) section unstitched for the drawstring channel before continuing to sew the remainder of each side seam.

9. **Make the lining:** Fold the lining fabric in half, right sides together, and machine sew the side seams from top to bottom, leaving a 4in (10cm) gap towards the bottom on one side only for turning the bag right side out in step 10.

10. **Join the bag outer and lining:** With the bag outer turned inside out and the lining turned right side out, place the lining inside the bag outer aligning the top edge and the side seams, and pin. Using a ¼in (6mm) seam allowance to reduce bulk, machine sew all the way around the top edge of the bag to sew the lining to the bag outer. Turn the bag right side out through the unsewn gap in the lining side seam. Press the seam at the top of the bag.

11. **Complete the drawstring channel:** Mark two lines across the bag to join the ends of the gaps left when sewing the side seams, ¾in (1.9cm) and 1¾in (4.4cm) from the top edge. Stitch around the bag on each line to make a channel for the drawstring. Take one drawstring cord and thread it through the channel on one side of the bag, then back through the channel on the other side of the bag, and knot the ends together. Repeat to insert the second drawstring cord, threading it through from the other side of the channel this time. Turn the bag inside out and slipstitch the gap in the lining closed. Turn the bag through to the right side.

12. **Make the drawstring flower trims:** Fold one 3½in (9cm) square of fabric in half, right sides together, and sew a ¼in (6mm) seam to make a tube. Press the seam open. Turn half of the tube right side out, so the fabric is doubled and the seam allowance hidden. With a double length of sewing thread, run small running stitches around the raw end of the tube. Slip the tube over the knotted end of the drawstring (with raw ends towards the knot) and gather up tightly (Fig 3). Take a few stitches through the cord and knot to finish off. Fold the tube down over the knot so it is hidden inside.

13. To add the 'stamens', pinch the open end of the tube to flatten it, stitch kogin thread through at the creases and leave loose. Pinch the end the other way and stitch another thread through. Hold all four ends of thread and knot together close to the end of the tube. Trim thread ends to finish.

Fig 3

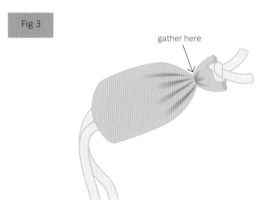

gather here

PHONE CASE

Shown as a case for your smartphone, this practical holder can be adapted for a range of different sized handheld electronic devices. I made mine using a traditional combination of white kogin thread on indigo blue 18-count evenweave, with a pretty batik patchwork cotton lining. It has a *bané* (snap or spring clasp) fastener, which is ideal for quick and easy access to your smartphone. Don't worry if your phone differs in size from mine – the type of fastener used is available in a variety of sizes, so the case can be easily adapted to suit the dimensions of your gadgets.

- One piece of indigo blue 18-count evenweave fabric 14 x 5¼in (35.6 x 13.3cm) for case outer

- One piece of batik patchwork cotton 14 x 5¼in (35.6 x 13.3cm) for lining

- One 4in (10cm)* *bané* (snap or spring clasp) fastener**

- Small hammer to close the snap fastener

- Sewing cotton to tone with fabrics

- Basic sewing kit (see Tools and Materials)

Snap fasteners are usually supplied in metric sizes only, so the imperial sizes given are approximate - just make sure that they are slightly smaller than the finished width of the case you are making. For making up the case in different sizes for other handheld devices, snap fasteners are available in a range of metric sizes: 8cm, 10cm, 12cm, 15cm and 30cm.

**This is sometimes called a flexible frame.*

FINISHED SIZE

6¼ x 3⅞in (16 x 9.8cm)

PATTERNS USED

(refer to Pattern Library)

Patterns 106 and 168

MAKING UP

1. Prepare and embroider the kogin panel: Oversew or zigzag the edges of the evenweave fabric (see Basic Techniques: Preparing Thread and Fabric). Find the centre of the fabric by folding it in half lengthwise and start stitching the kogin from here, referring to Basic Techniques: Stitching Kogin and the diagram of the finished stitching (see Fig 1). I made my case to fit a smartphone, so it will be handled a lot, and therefore I chose simple kogin and Nanbu hishizashi patterns that don't have long stitches on the right side of the work. Pattern 168 is particularly hard-wearing, so I used nine horizontal bands of it on the back of the case, finishing the front panel embroidery with one horizontal band of the same pattern at the bottom edge. Once the stitching is complete, press lightly from the back of the kogin.

TIP

Pattern 106 is a continuous pattern. For pattern 168, rather than finish off your thread and restart it for each pattern band, 'travel' the thread up the side of your panel within the area that will become the seam allowance.

Fig 1

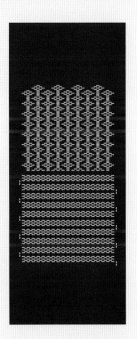

2. **Sew up the side seams and add the lining:** Fold the kogin panel in half, right sides together. Measure 1in (2.5cm) from the top edge on each side and place pins to mark the area for the snap fastener channel (see Fig 2). Machine sew the side seams from the pins with a ⅜in (1cm) seam allowance, starting and finishing with a few backstitches each time. Press the side seam allowance open all the way up to the top edge of the case, including the unsewn area.

3. Fold the lining fabric in half, right sides together, and machine sew the side seams from top to bottom, leaving a 3in (7.6cm) gap towards the bottom on one side only for turning the case right side out in step 4. Press seams open.

4. Place the case outer (which is still inside out) inside the lining so the right sides of the lining and the kogin panel are facing each other, and pin and tack (baste) around the top edge. Machine sew right around the top, slightly less than ⅜in (1cm) from the edge, slightly overlapping the ends of the stitching, starting and finishing with a few backstitches. Note: the phone case is too narrow for a sewing machine free arm, so it has to be sewn with the machine foot against the inside of the phone case (Fig 3). Turn the case right side out through the unsewn gap in the lining side seam, and finger press the seam around the top edge. You can now slipstitch the gap in the lining closed.

5. **Complete the snap fastener channel:** Tack (baste) around the top of the case, about 1in (2.5cm) from the edge, then machine sew to make a channel for the snap fastener, stitching from the inside as in step 4 and linking the base of the gaps in the case sides. Remove the tacking (basting) stitches.

6. **Add the snap fastener to finish the phone case:** Turn the case through to the right side. Slide the snap fastener into the channel at both sides of the case at the same time, wriggling it in until the open ends come out at the other side (Fig 4). Bring the ends of the snap fastener together and insert the pin (supplied with the fastener) to hold it together, tapping lightly with a small hammer to drive it home.

Fig 2

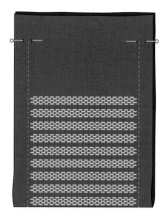

Fig 3

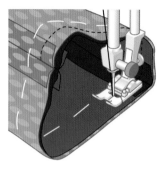

Fig 4

TIP

When inserting the snap fastener into the channel, be careful that it doesn't get caught in the side seams – use something thin and flat, like a small screwdriver or metal nail file, to hold down the seam allowance as it exits the channel.

MAKING UP THE CASE IN DIFFERENT SIZES

1. Measure your chosen gadget: To make your case to perfectly fit your electronic devices if they differ in size from mine, start by measuring your chosen gadget, making a note of its length, width and depth. Remember that even the slimmest gadget has depth, and you will need to allow for the flat case to be a little bigger than your gadget or it will be too small. Add the length to the depth for the absolute minimum finished case length, and the width to the depth for the minimum finished case width. It can also be handy to take total measurements around your gadget, using a tape measure wrapped right around to measure the total length and width, then dividing by 2 (for the case width only) to check you have added up correctly.

2. Use these measurements to work out the size needed for the finished fit of the case outer panel, allowing a little extra for ease - ½-¾in (1.3-1.9cm) - to allow for the extra thickness of the kogin and any slight pulling in of the fabric when the kogin is stitched. Add on ⅜in (1cm) for seam allowances and cut out the case outer and lining panel fabrics. (To see how I worked out the fabric requirements for my smartphone, see Working Example.)

TIP

If in doubt, cut your bag panel a little larger to allow for any errors (far better than making the case too small); you can fold the cut fabric around your gadget before stitching and make any necessary adjustments at that stage.

Working Example

My phone measures 2⁹⁄₁₆in (6.5cm) wide x 5⅛in (13cm) long x ½in (1.3cm) deep (if you keep your gadget in a protective transparent high-impact case, as I do, measure it *in* that case). So my finished case needs to be at least 3¼in (8.3cm) wide x 5⅝in (14.3cm) long (excluding the channel for the snap fastener).

To work out the total length of my kogin panel, I need to start with (length + depth) x 2 = (5⅛ + ½in (13 + 1.3cm)) x 2 = 11¼ (28.6cm). I need to add 1in (2.5cm) to each end of the panel length, to allow for making the fastener channel, therefore 11¼in (28.6cm) + 2in (5cm) = 13¼in (33.7cm). I added an extra ¾in (1.9cm) to the cut length to allow a little ease, so the snap fastener would have enough room to close flat when the phone was in the case = 14in (35.6cm).

For the width, the size of snap fastener closest to my required finished case size is 3⅞in (9.8cm), then I need to add ¾in (1.9cm) for the side seam allowances = 4⅝in (11.7cm). It will need to be a little wider, however, to allow some extra for the thickness of the kogin stitches and the lining fabric - if the case is very tight, I won't be able to get the phone in and out easily - so I rounded up the cut width to 5¼in (13.3cm).

So the total size for cutting both the kogin panel and the lining fabric in this instance is 14 x 5¼in (35.6 x 13.3cm), which allows a ⅜in (1cm) seam allowance at the sides and around the top.

BUTTONS, BROOCHES
AND BOBBLES

Buttons are a very popular way to show off a small piece of kogin. With self-cover button kits, assembly couldn't be simpler – button blank and backing simply snap together to catch the embroidered top fabric in between. Available in packs of various sizes, self-cover button kits generally come with a template for cutting the fabric to size and a setting tool. Start with a large button and progress to making smaller ones as you become more dexterous at button assembly. When you have all the buttons you need, you can make a few brooches or hair bobbles using the same technique.

- Oddments of evenweave fabrics, 20-count and finer*

- Oddments of kogin and six-strand embroidery threads

- Button blanks from a self-cover button kit

- Small hammer or setting tool**

- Impact adhesive

- Basic sewing kit (see Tools and Materials)

Thicker fabrics won't tuck in so readily, so I recommend using 20-count or finer evenweave fabrics, even going as fine as 32-count for really tiny buttons.

**If you plan to make lots of buttons, a button-making machine will make the job even simpler.*

FINISHED SIZE

Varies according to the size of your button blanks; mine range from ¾–1¾in (2–4.5cm) in diameter.

PATTERNS USED

(refer to Pattern Library)

Any of the patterns from Small Continuous Patterns or smaller Motifs would be suitable

MAKING UP A BUTTON

1 . Prepare the fabric for stitching: Using the template from the button kit, use a fabric marker or pencil to draw a circle on your chosen evenweave fabric. If you do not have a template, draw a circle that measures approx. twice the diameter of the button. *Do not cut out the circle before beginning the kogin or your fabric will stretch and fray as you stitch.* For such a small project, oversewing or zigzagging the edge of your fabric oddment to prevent fraying is not absolutely necessary, but if you are stitching several kogin buttons on one larger piece of fabric, it is most definitely a good idea.

2 . Choose and stitch your kogin pattern: Referring to the Pattern Library and using the photograph of my finished buttons as a guide, select a suitable kogin pattern: remember, even very simple designs can look effective as buttons.

3 . Find the centre of the marked circle by folding the fabric in quarters, then start stitching, referring to Basic Techniques: Stitching Kogin. Motifs look best centred on the button front; for continuous designs, stitch the kogin over the edge of the button front but stop slightly short of the button back to avoid any unnecessary bulk. Once the stitching is complete, press lightly from the back of the kogin and then cut out the kogin circle along the marked line.

4 . Assemble the button: Run a little adhesive around the back of the button blank, inside the dip. Centre the kogin circle on the front of the button blank and fold the edges to the back, pushing them down into the glue and working your way around the button. Once all the fabric is folded over and held in place, push the button back into position using the setting tool provided with the kit (or a small hammer) as necessary.

MAKING UP A BROOCH OR HAIR BOBBLE

1 . Make a brooch: These can be made following the steps for making a button; simply remove the wire loop from the back plate of the button blank and thread on a safety pin before replacing the wire. Alternatively, invest in a brooch kit.

2 . Make a hair bobble: Follow the steps for making a button, but simply remove the wire loop from the back plate of the button blank and thread on an elastic hair tie before replacing the wire.

FRAMED PICTURES

Small samples are a good way to practise stitching kogin patterns and, with the availability of inexpensive ready-made photograph frames, they can easily be turned into quickly made gifts. For my framed sample collection, I chose simple oak-effect photo frames made for 4in (10cm) square prints. Although the 18-count evenweave fabric oddments I selected are in three different colours, I stitched the kogin patterns in pure white kogin thread to make a coordinating set. Simply find your frame, then stitch your kogin to fit.

- ▶ A small photo frame of your choice
- ▶ A piece of 18-count evenweave fabric to fit your chosen frame
- ▶ One 19¾yd (18m) skein of kogin thread
- ▶ Iron-on interfacing the same size as your fabric
- ▶ Basic sewing kit (see Tools and Materials)

FINISHED SIZE

Varies depending on the size of your chosen frame

PATTERNS USED

(refer to Pattern Library)

Patterns 78, 120 and 227

MAKING UP

1. **Prepare your fabric:** If there is glass in the frame, carefully remove it. Measure the inside of the frame and cut your fabric a little larger to mark the working area. If the frame has a mount that will mask part of the fabric, make a note of its width: your kogin doesn't need to extend very far behind the mount – ⅛in (3mm) is ample. Oversew or zigzag the edges of your evenweave fabric (see Basic Techniques: Preparing Thread and Fabric).

2. **Stitch the kogin sample:** Referring to Basic Techniques: Stitching Kogin, stitch the kogin pattern of your choosing. Lightly press the finished kogin panel from the back.

3. **Assemble the picture frame:** Following the manufacturer's instructions, iron on the interfacing to the back of the kogin panel. Using the outer edge of the mount as a guide, trim the interfaced kogin panel so it fits snugly inside the frame. Reassemble the frame, restoring the glass panel if you choose to.

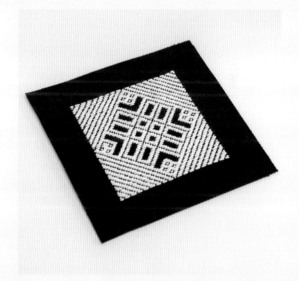

PATTERN
LIBRARY

There are over 230 charted patterns for you to use as you wish. I have arranged them into sections according to pattern type, e.g. motifs or diagonal borders and frames, starting with smaller, easier designs and working up to a section dedicated to large patterns. There is also a section on Nanbu hishizashi motifs.

Many of the patterns have traditional names often given in Tsugaru-Ben, the local dialect around the Hirosaki area where kogin originates from. These have been included with a translation alongside. Each design also has a number, to help you identify patterns, particularly where they are named as a group rather than individually.

On the charts, the light grey background grids represent the fabric threads and the coloured lines are the stitches. Remember to carefully count your fabric threads for accurate stitching. You may find it useful to make a photocopy of the chart you are working from and mark across completed rows with a highlighter pen as you stitch.

PATTERN NAMES AND THEIR MEANINGS

The basic patterns of kogin are called *modoko*. Larger *modoko* patterns often use elements of smaller ones as their basic units. By combining *modoko*, larger patterns are created, often with the addition of *ito nagare* (thread flow) diagonal patterns to make frames. It is thought that there are more than 500 pattern combinations. Continuous (or all-over) patterns are called *sōzashi* (whole embroidery). The basic Nanbu hishizashi diamond motifs are called *kataco* (small shape). Many kogin and Nanbu hishizashi patterns share the same names. Here are a few examples:

uroko **(fish) scale** Also snake or dragon scale: represents defeat of evil, or good luck with money.

kumo (zashi) **spider (stitch)** Denotes a happy encounter as the spider's thread catches good luck.

komakura **small pillow** Refers to the high pillow once used in traditional hairstyles.

bekozashi **cow stitch** So called because the pattern looks like a cow's footprint.

kikkō **hexagon** In Japan hexagons represent turtle shells, signifying long life as the turtle is a symbol of longevity.

take no fushi **bamboo joint** Represents fortuity as the bamboo is a symbol of good luck.

ichimatsu A check pattern named after Ichimatsu, a kabuki (traditional Japanese theatre) actor who used this pattern in the clothing he wore.

fukube **gourd** Indicates good luck, good health and prosperity.

soroban **abacus** A sign of wealth and prosperity.

uma no kutsuwa **horse bit** A talisman against evil.

MOTIFS

Individual named motifs form the building blocks of traditional kogin patterns, included in the 40 basic patterns or *modoko* identified by the Hirosaki Kogin Lab's research. Different kogin stitchers seem to have had variations on these too, so as many as possible have been included in this section. They can all be adapted to all-over patterns either by simple tessellation or by adding links, borders or frames between the individual motifs (see Basic Techniques: Designing Kogin). The floral plum blossom motifs are popular modern patterns. Motifs may be stitched with or without the single stitch at the top and bottom; it is the more modern approach to include them, while traditional kogin often omits these tiny stitches. The figures given in brackets at the end of each pattern caption indicate the number of threads for a pattern repeat, to help you to plan your design.

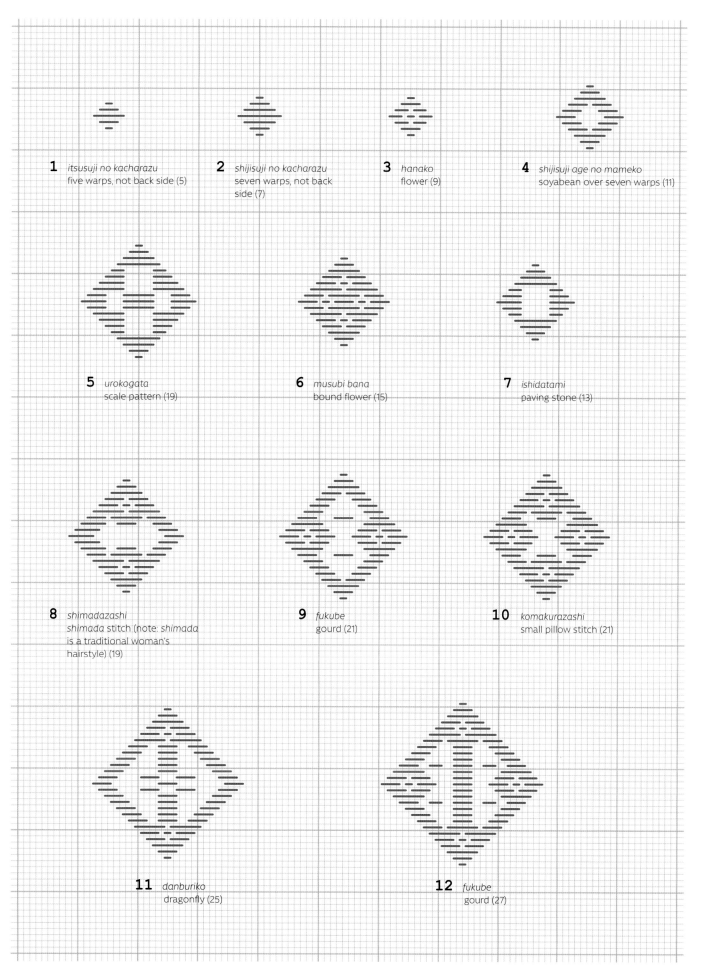

1 *itsusuji no kacharazu*
five warps, not back side (5)

2 *shijisuji no kacharazu*
seven warps, not back
side (7)

3 *hanako*
flower (9)

4 *shijisuji age no mameko*
soyabean over seven warps (11)

5 *urokogata*
scale pattern (19)

6 *musubi bana*
bound flower (15)

7 *ishidatami*
paving stone (13)

8 *shimadazashi*
shimada stitch (note: *shimada*
is a traditional woman's
hairstyle) (19)

9 *fukube*
gourd (21)

10 *komakurazashi*
small pillow stitch (21)

11 *danburiko*
dragonfly (25)

12 *fukube*
gourd (27)

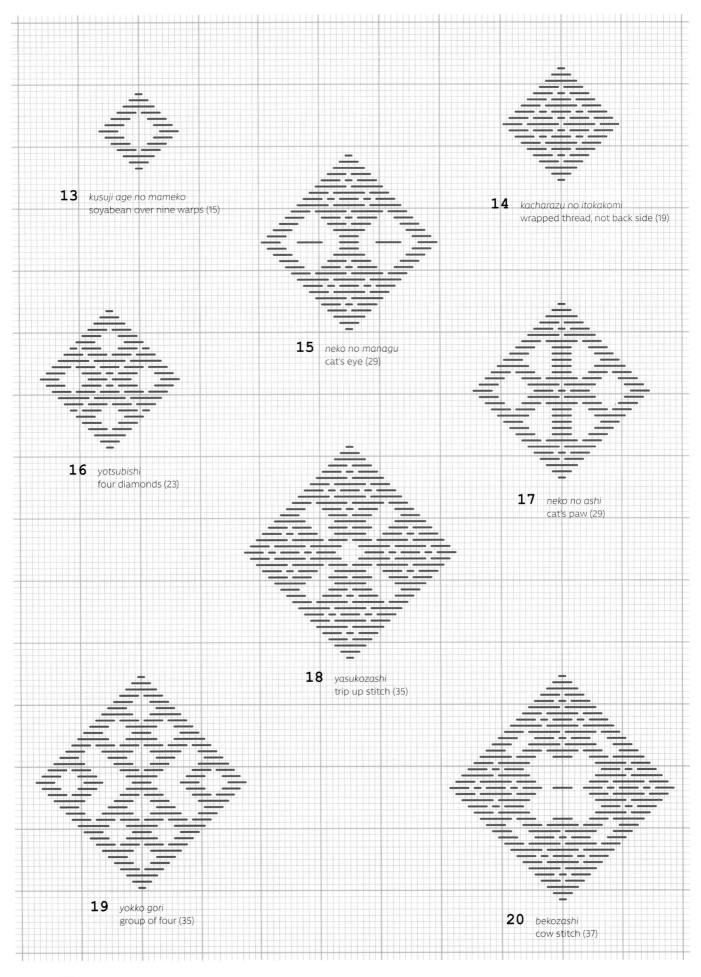

13 *kusuji age no mameko*
soyabean over nine warps (15)

14 *kacharazu no itokakomi*
wrapped thread, not back side (19)

15 *neko no managu*
cat's eye (29)

16 *yotsubishi*
four diamonds (23)

17 *neko no ashi*
cat's paw (29)

18 *yasukozashi*
trip up stitch (35)

19 *yokko gori*
group of four (35)

20 *bekozashi*
cow stitch (37)

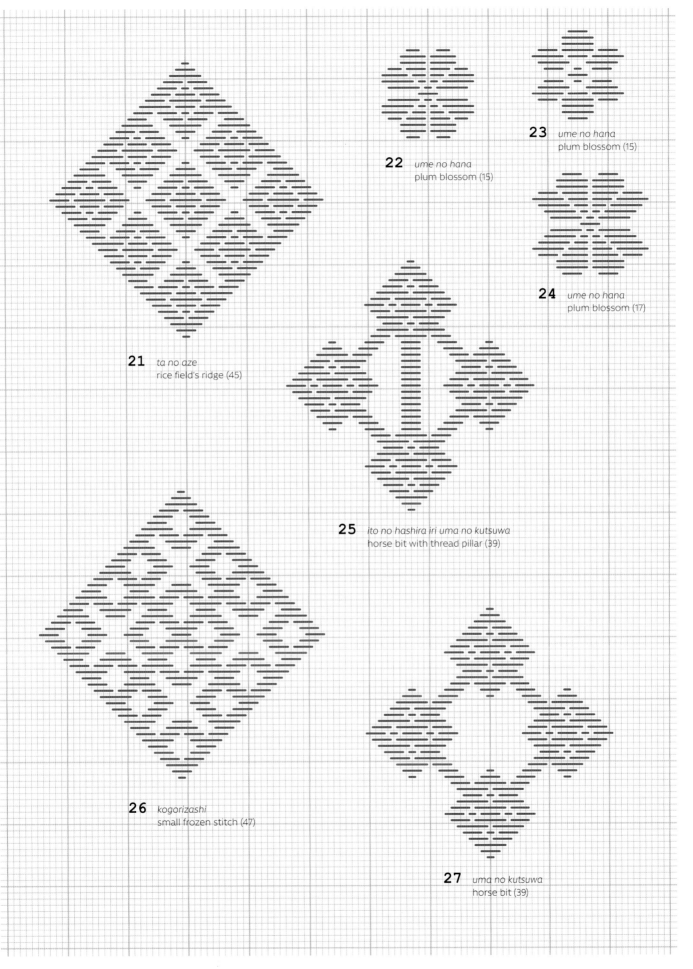

22 *ume no hana*
plum blossom (15)

23 *ume no hana*
plum blossom (15)

21 *ta no aze*
rice field's ridge (45)

24 *ume no hana*
plum blossom (17)

25 *ito no hashira iri uma no kutsuwa*
horse bit with thread pillar (39)

26 *kogorizashi*
small frozen stitch (47)

27 *uma no kutsuwa*
horse bit (39)

28 *hana tsunagi*
linked flowers (33)

29 *sayagata*
saya brocade pattern (51)

30 *tekonako*
butterfly (33)

31 *tomarazu*
endless (51)

32 *urokogata*
scale pattern (37)

33 *kumozashi*
spider stitch (55)

34 *idowaku*
well frame (33)

35 *hanako no hashira iri*
flower with column (55)

36 *kurumi gara*
walnut shell (39)

37 *yabane zashi*
arrow stitch (51)

38 *kawari sayagata*
saya brocade variation (71)

39 *kinone no kikurake*
tree root's bend (33)

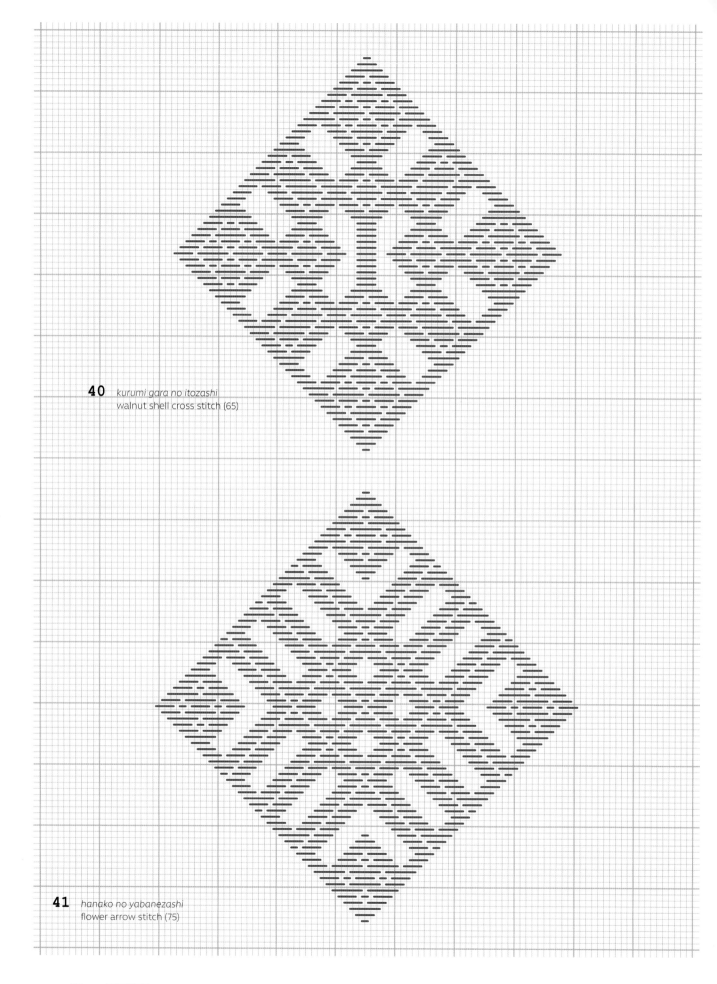

40 *kurumi gara no itozashi*
walnut shell cross stitch (65)

41 *hanako no yabanezashi*
flower arrow stitch (75)

42 *yasukozashi*
trip up stitch (43)

43 *yotsu mameko*
four beans (39)

44 *tekona no yabane zashi*
butterfly arrow stitch (103)

SMALL CONTINUOUS PATTERNS

These were traditionally stitched at the bottom of the bodice on *koginu*, hidden by the obi sash when worn, or as hard-wearing shoulder patterns. Others were used in large kogin designs, to surround the motifs to create larger patterns. Today, continuous patterns are popular for smaller projects as they are very easy to stitch with just a few rows in each pattern repeat. Small continuous patterns for kogin (purple charts) are ideal for stitching within an outline like a simple circle or heart. Nanbu hishizashi continuous patterns (orange charts) are usually related to the individual hishizashi lozenge patterns (see Nanbu Hishizashi Motifs). Some are similar to the *hitomezashi* (one stitch) sashiko patterns of Yamagata Prefecture, or the counted sashiko stitched on headscarves from Akita Prefecture.

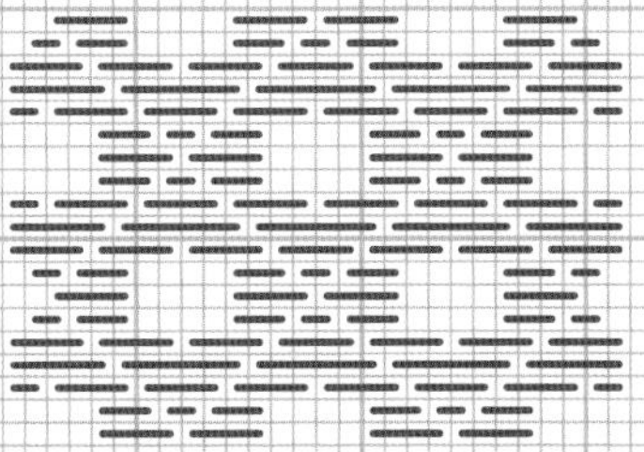

45 *ishidatami*
stone pavement

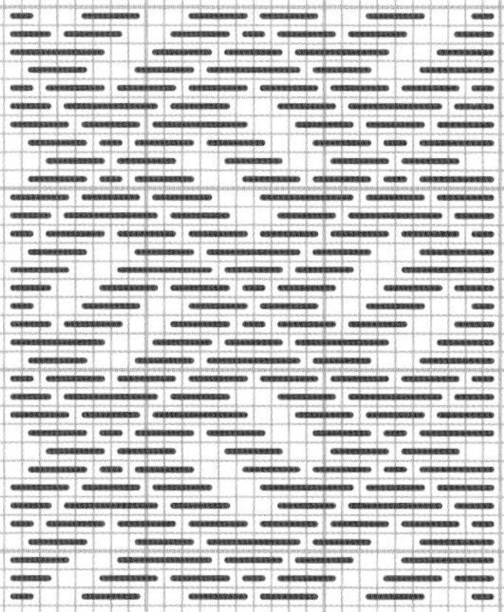

46 *so mōyō*
continuous pattern

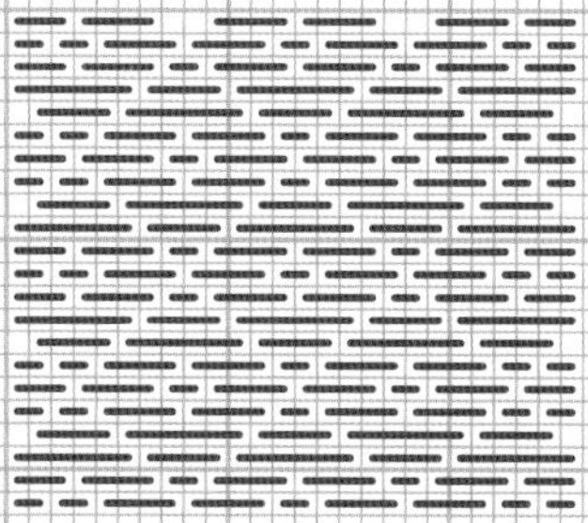

47 *hanako*
flower

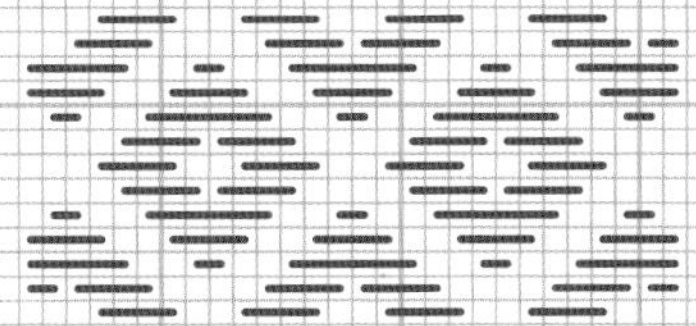

48 *hanako*
flower

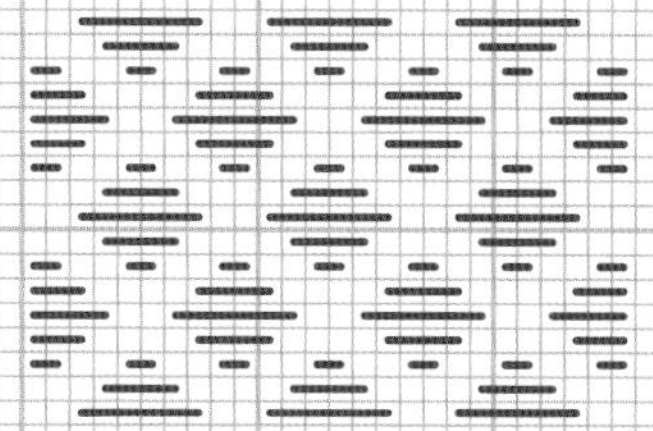

49 *itsujiage*
over five warps

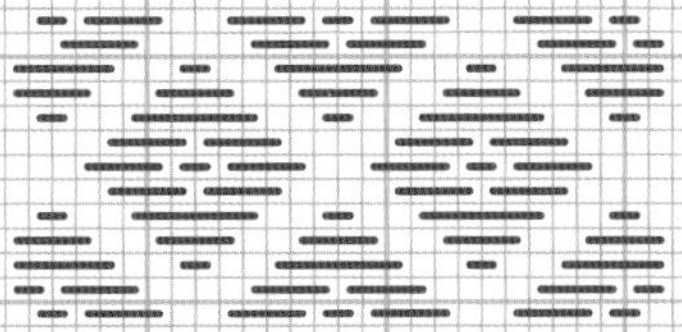

50 *hanako*
flower

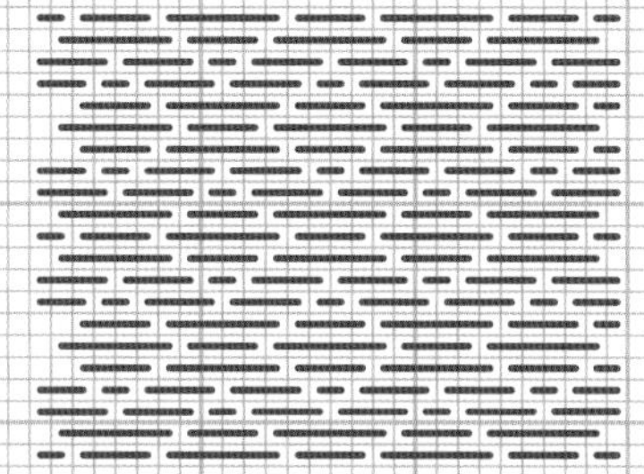

51 *kacharazu no itoire*
not backside of threads

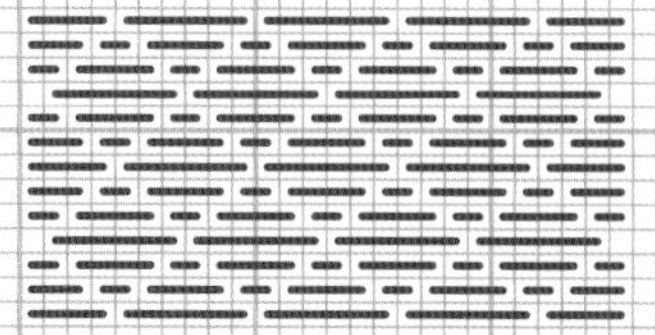

52 *itsujiage*
over five warps

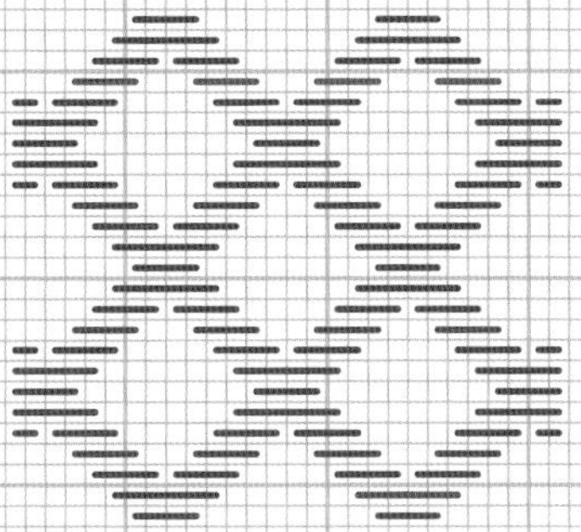

53 *kusujiage*
over nine warps

54 *shijisujiage*
over seven warps

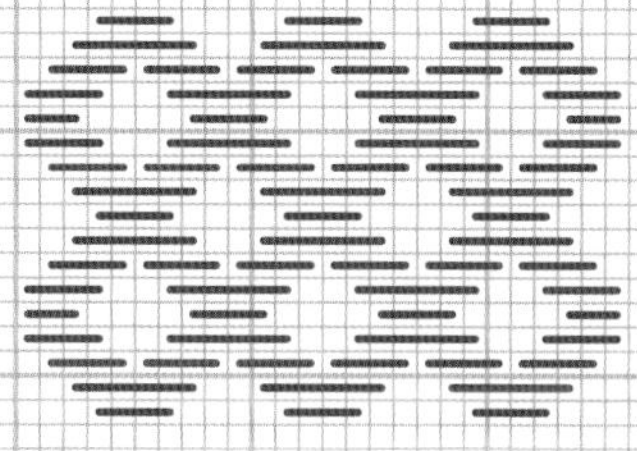

55 *itsujiage*
over five warps

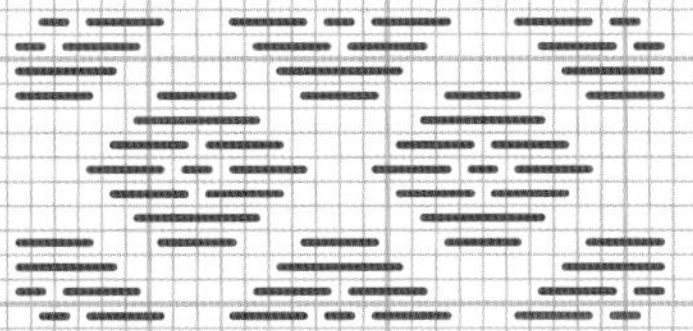

56 *hanako*
flower

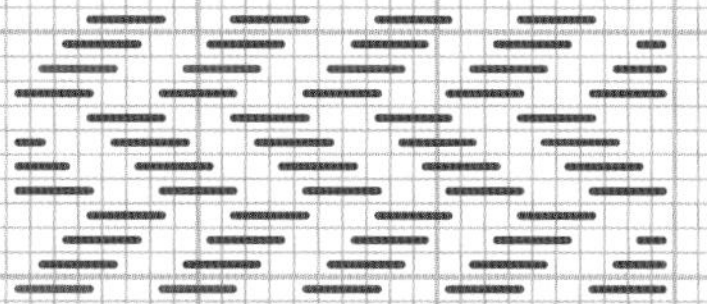

57 *sugiha*
cedar leaf

58 *ito nagare*
thread flow

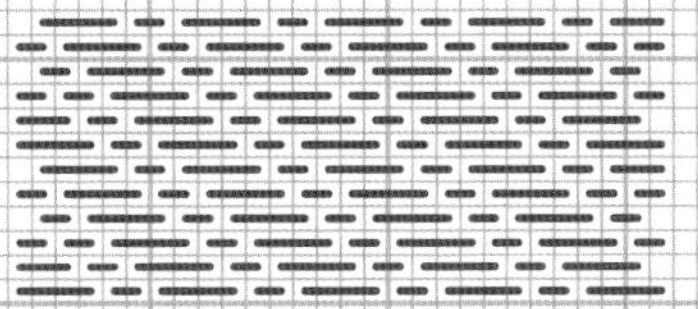

59 *ito nagare*
thread flow

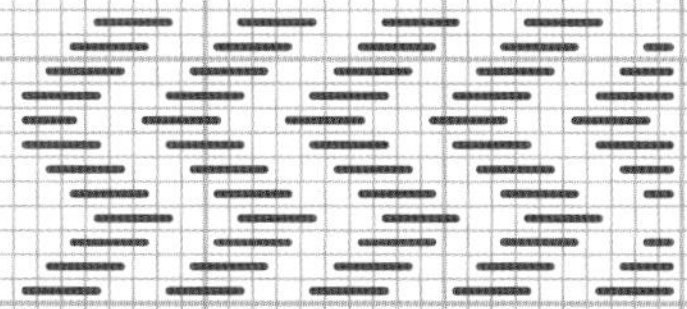

60 *nokogiri no ha*
saw's teeth

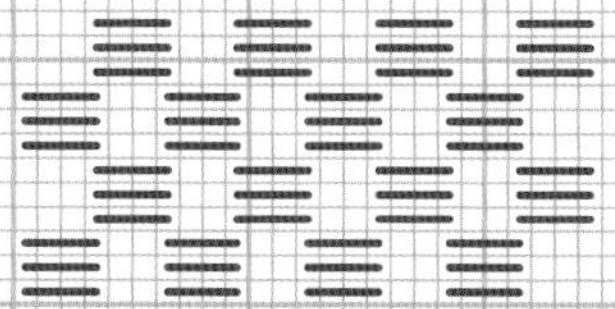

61 *ichimatsu*
Ichimatsu's check pattern

Patterns 62–64 *fune no ho ship's sail*

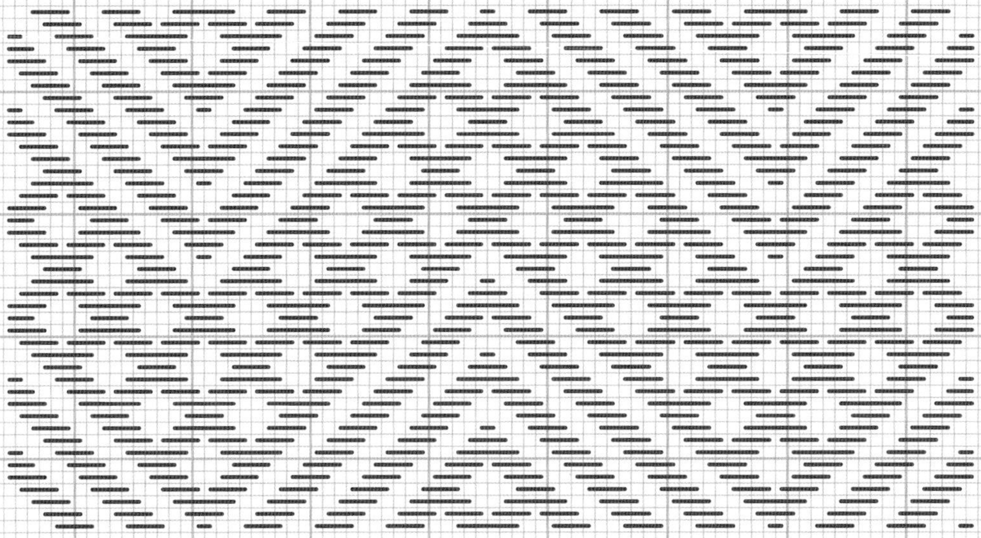

62

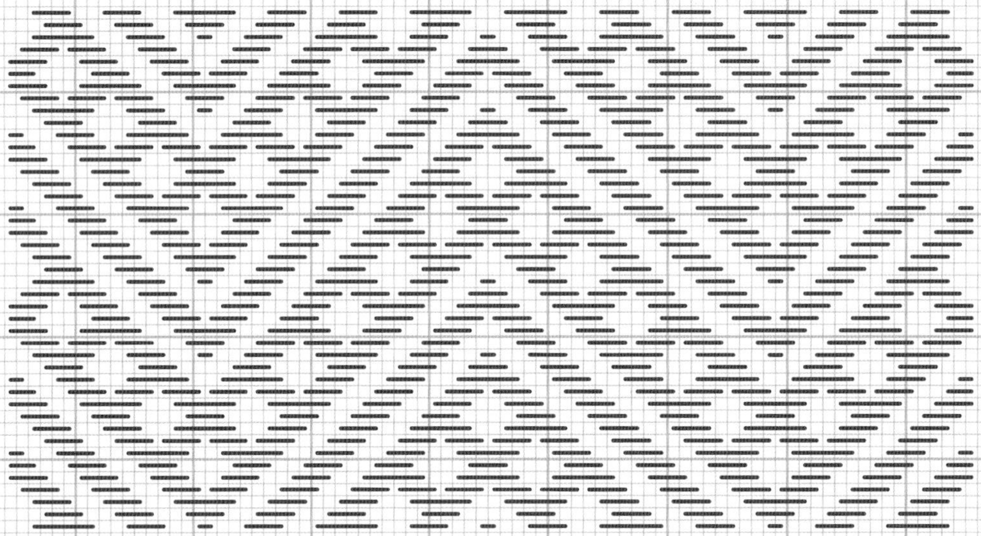

63

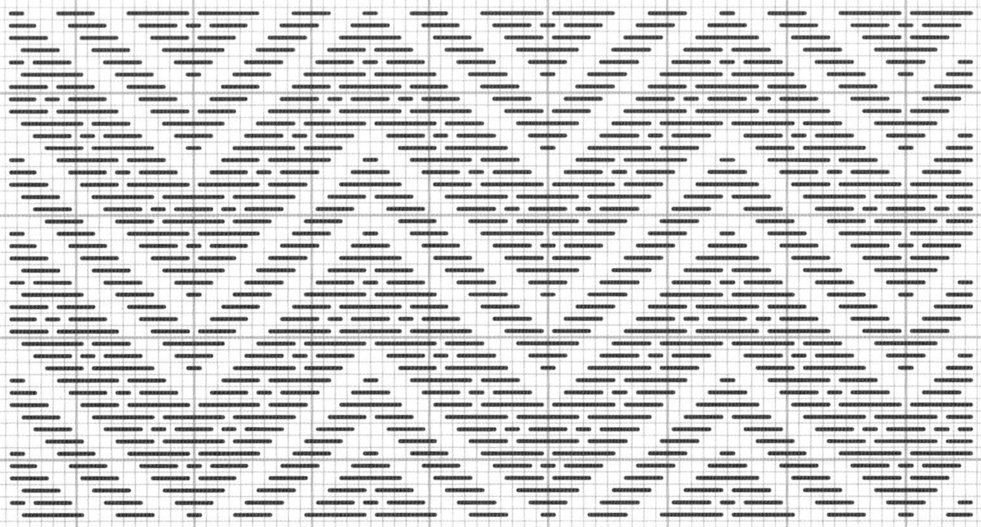

64

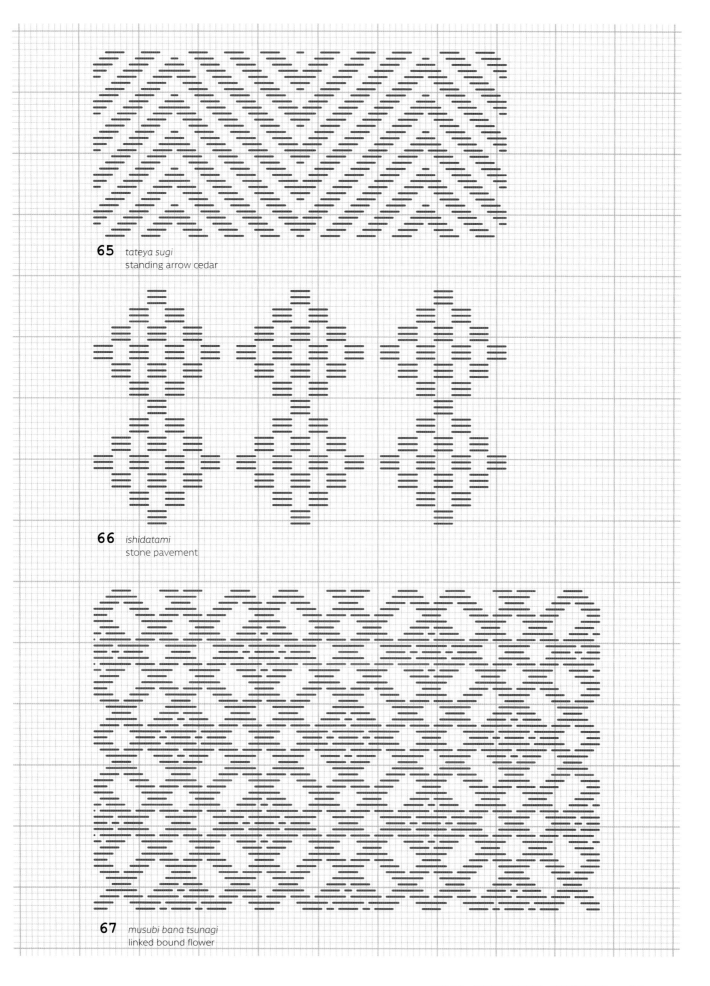

65 *tateya sugi*
standing arrow cedar

66 *ishidatami*
stone pavement

67 *musubi bana tsunagi*
linked bound flower

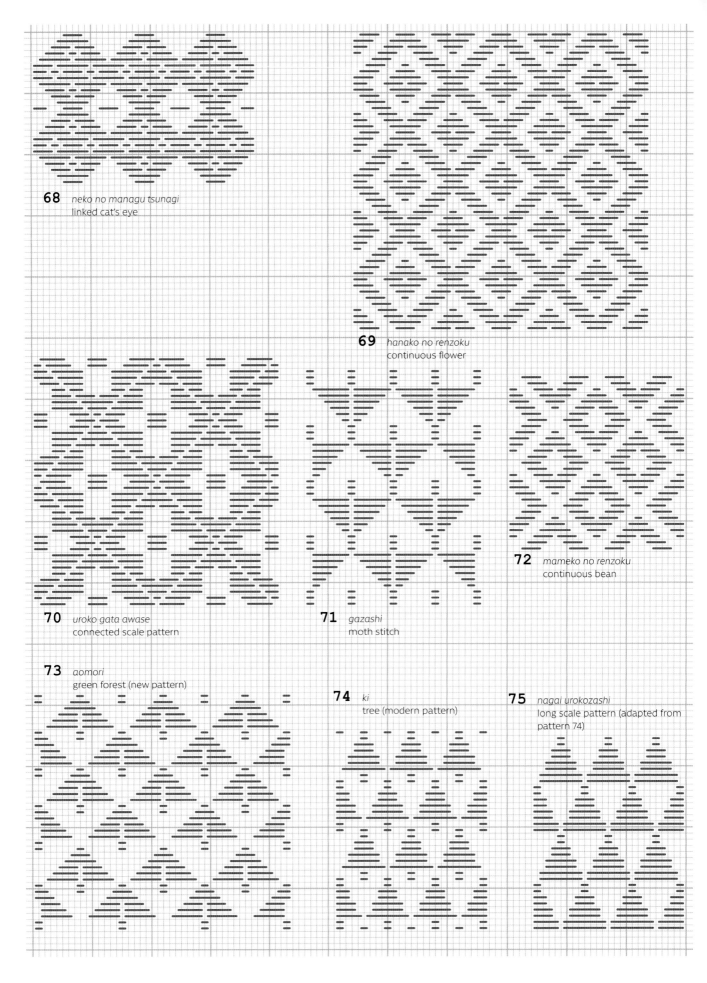

68 *neko no managu tsunagi*
linked cat's eye

69 *hanako no renzoku*
continuous flower

70 *uroko gata awase*
connected scale pattern

71 *gazashi*
moth stitch

72 *mameko no renzoku*
continuous bean

73 *aomori*
green forest (new pattern)

74 *ki*
tree (modern pattern)

75 *nagai urokozashi*
long scale pattern (adapted from
pattern 74)

76 *sayagata*
saya brocade pattern

77 *sayagata sanponhashira*
three pillar saya brocade pattern

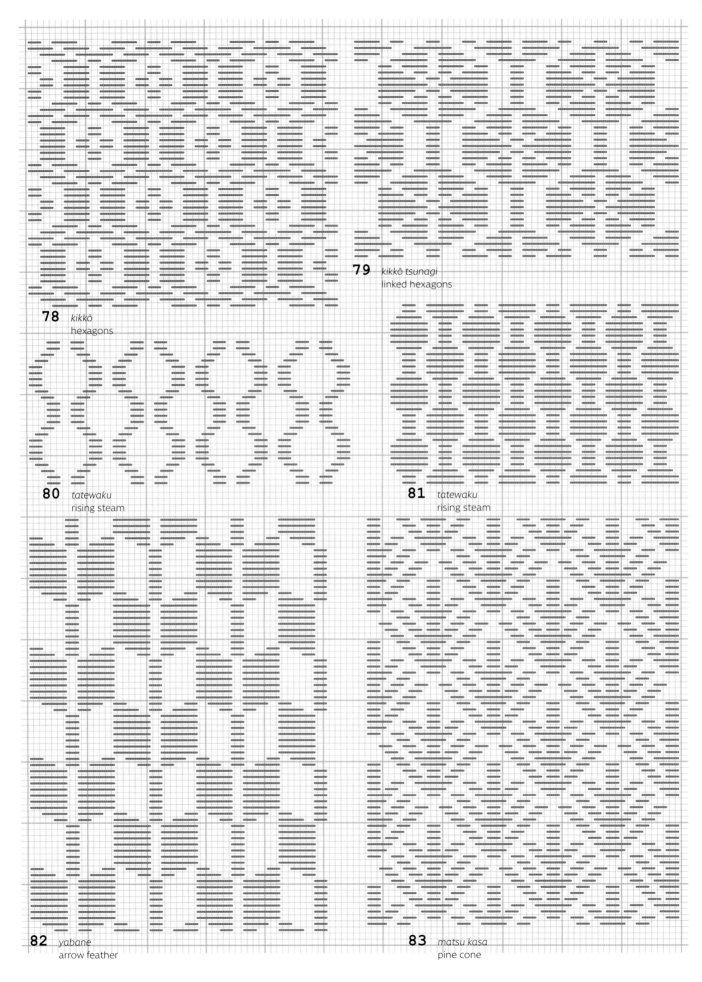

79 *kikkō tsunagi*
linked hexagons

78 *kikkō*
hexagons

80 *tatewaku*
rising steam

81 *tatewaku*
rising steam

82 *yabane*
arrow feather

83 *matsu kasa*
pine cone

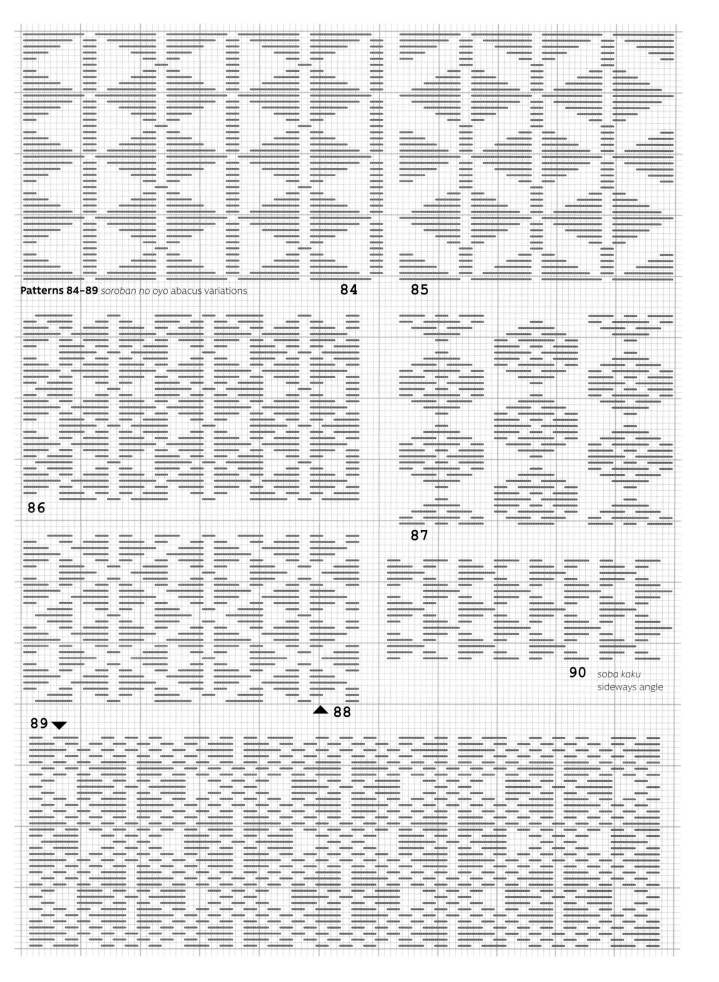

Patterns 84–89 *soroban no oyo* abacus variations

84

85

86

87

▲ **88**

89 ▼

90 *soba kaku*
sideways angle

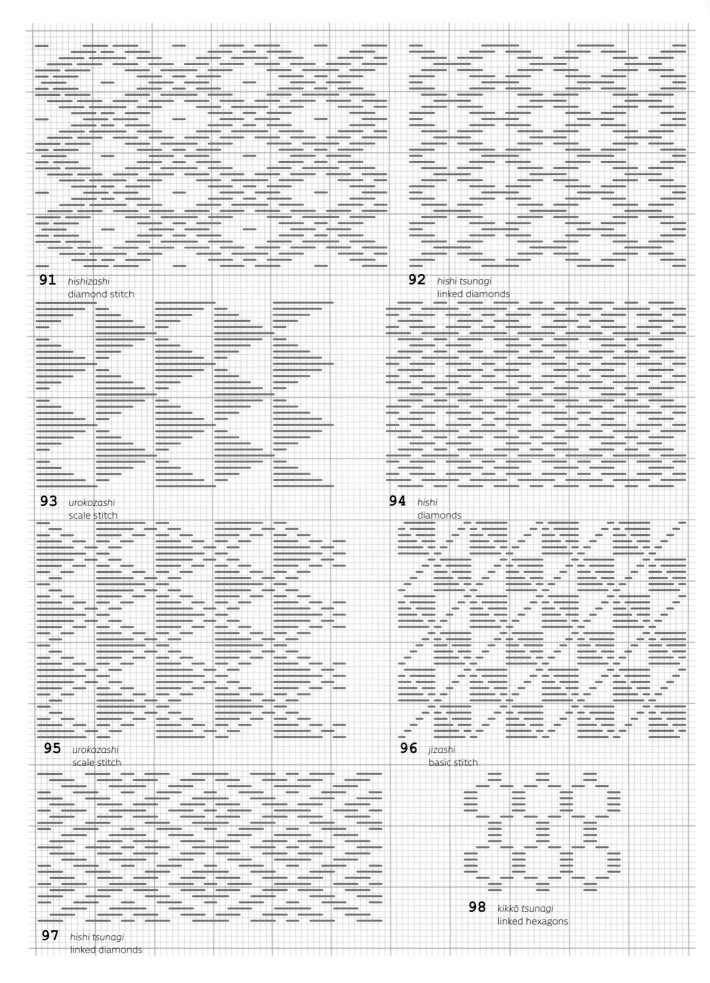

91 *hishizashi*
diamond stitch

92 *hishi tsunagi*
linked diamonds

93 *urokozashi*
scale stitch

94 *hishi*
diamonds

95 *urokozashi*
scale stitch

96 *jizashi*
basic stitch

98 *kikkō tsunagi*
linked hexagons

97 *hishi tsunagi*
linked diamonds

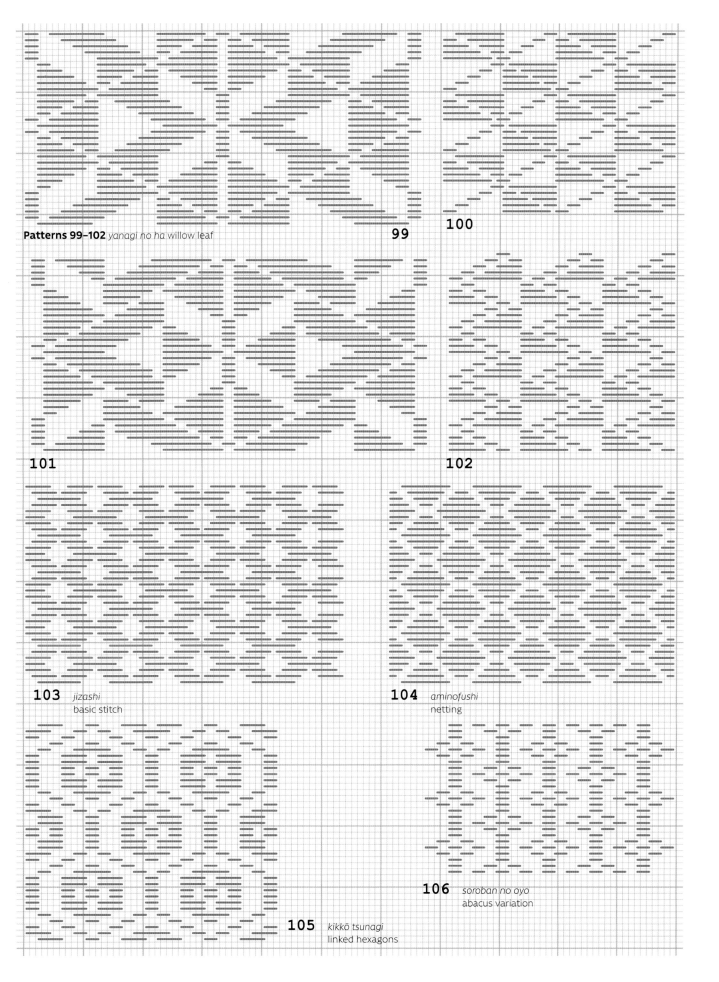

Patterns 99–102 *yanagi no ha* willow leaf

99

100

101

102

103 *jizashi*
basic stitch

104 *aminofushi*
netting

106 *soroban no oyo*
abacus variation

105 *kikkō tsunagi*
linked hexagons

MOTIF ARRANGEMENTS

Many all-over patterns repeat individual *modoko* (motifs) in a grid arrangement, with just a gap of one thread in between or in more complex diagonal frames. The use of grids is seen in Higashi and Nishi kogin areas. For more variety, combine different motifs with the same number of stitches; or use two differently sized motifs, infilling the gap around the smaller one with a small continuous pattern or a tiny frame; or alternate a single motif with a small continuous pattern in each grid 'cell'. Motifs can also be joined with *hashira* (thread pillars) or *ito nagare* (thread flow) diagonal lines. On the last row of the stitched sample, the single grid frame has been stitched in a different shade, but traditionally the same thread colour is used across the pattern. For more advice, see Basic Techniques: Working with Multiple Colours.

107 *neko no ashi*
cat's paw

108 *neko no ashi de narabeta*
arranged cat's paw

109 *neko no ashi no ito nagare*
cat's paw thread flow

110 *kakomi*
enclosure

111 *kakomi*
enclosure

112 *oru*
weave

113

114

115

116 *uma no kutsuwa kin iri no oyo*
horse bit diagonal variation

▲ **117** *tekona no oyo*
butterfly variation

▼ **118** *urokogata no oyo*
scale pattern variation

119 *uma no kutsuwa no renzoku*
continuous horse bit

120 *musubi bana no ito hashira*
thread pillar bound flower

121 *musubi bana no renzoku*
continuous bound flower

▲ **122** *misujiage sanbon no oyo*
three times three threads variation

▼ **123** *misujiage sanbon no oyo*
three times three threads variation

▲ **124** *shimada zashi no musubi bana nagare*
shimada stitch and bound flower thread flow

▼**125** *uma no kutsuwa mameko tsunagi*
horse bit and linked bean

DIAGONAL BORDERS AND FRAMES

Diagonal borders (pink charts) can be used to frame individual motifs or small continuous patterns. Many link small *modoko* in different ways. Repeated diagonal borders in V- and W-shaped configurations are typical of the lower bodice sections of Mishima kogin jackets. In Higashi and Nishi kogin, diagonal borders are often adjusted to fit a central design. Most patterns have long descriptive names, so I have used their group name *ito nagare* (thread flow) for simplicity. Some diagonal border designs have specific ways to turn the corners when used as frames (green charts), particularly the complex *sayagata* (saya brocade) pattern. These *kakomi* (enclosures) can be enlarged or reduced to fit; central square spaces can be filled in with smaller *modoko* patterns and rectangular areas can be filled with basic *ito nagare* (thread flow), pattern 126.

Patterns 126–135
ito nagare thread flow

126
127
128
129
130
131
132
133
134
135

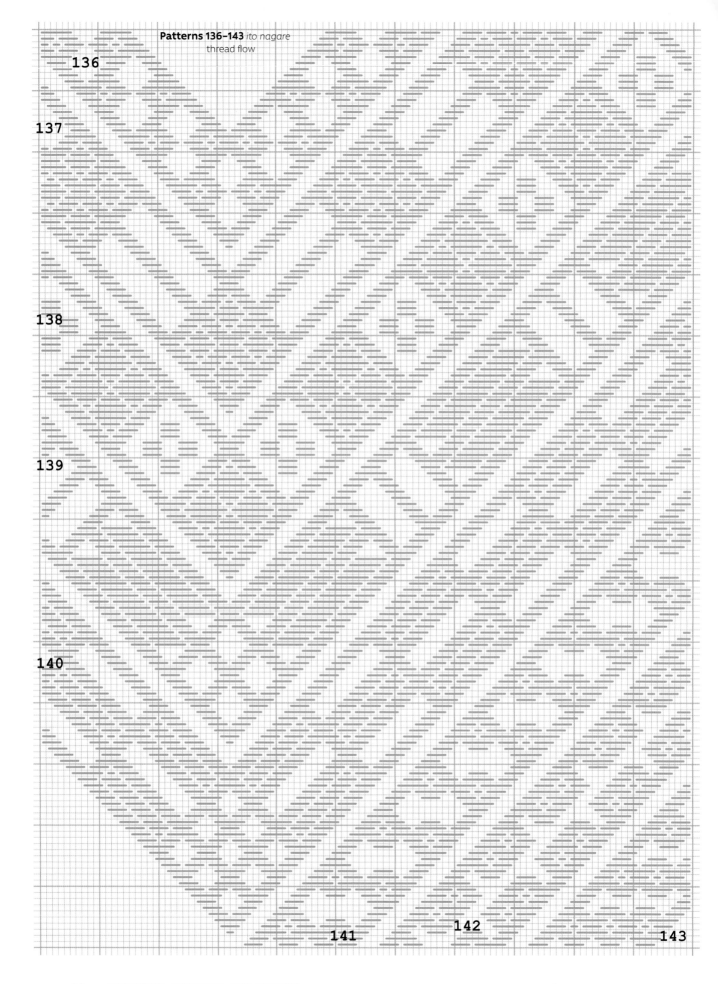

Patterns 136–143 *ito nagare*
thread flow

136

137

138

139

140

141

142

143

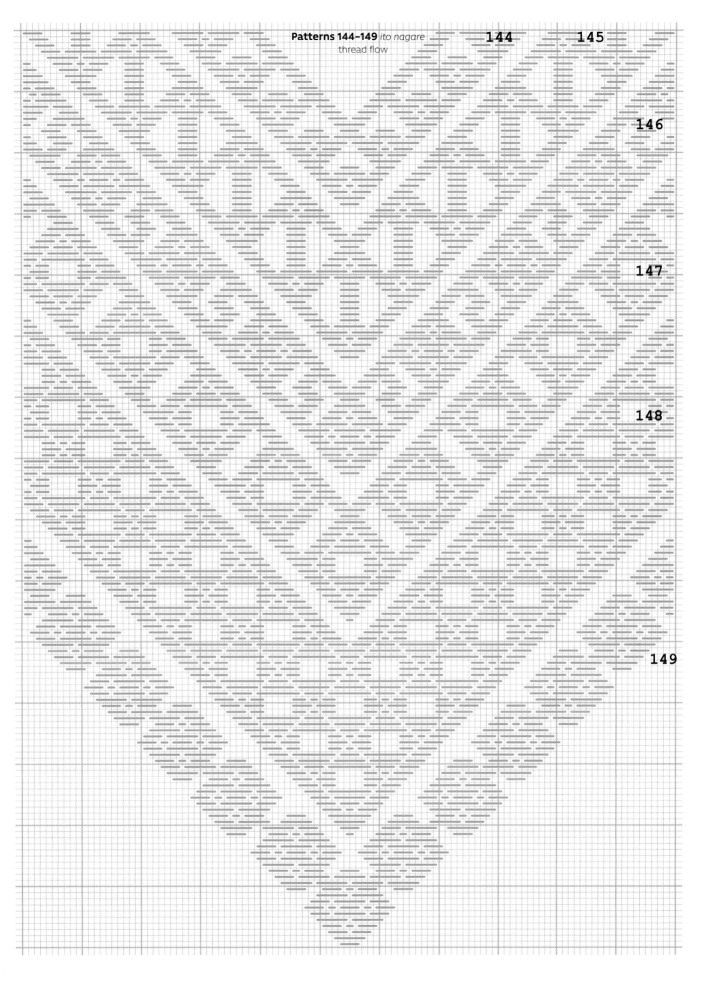

144   145

146

147

148

149

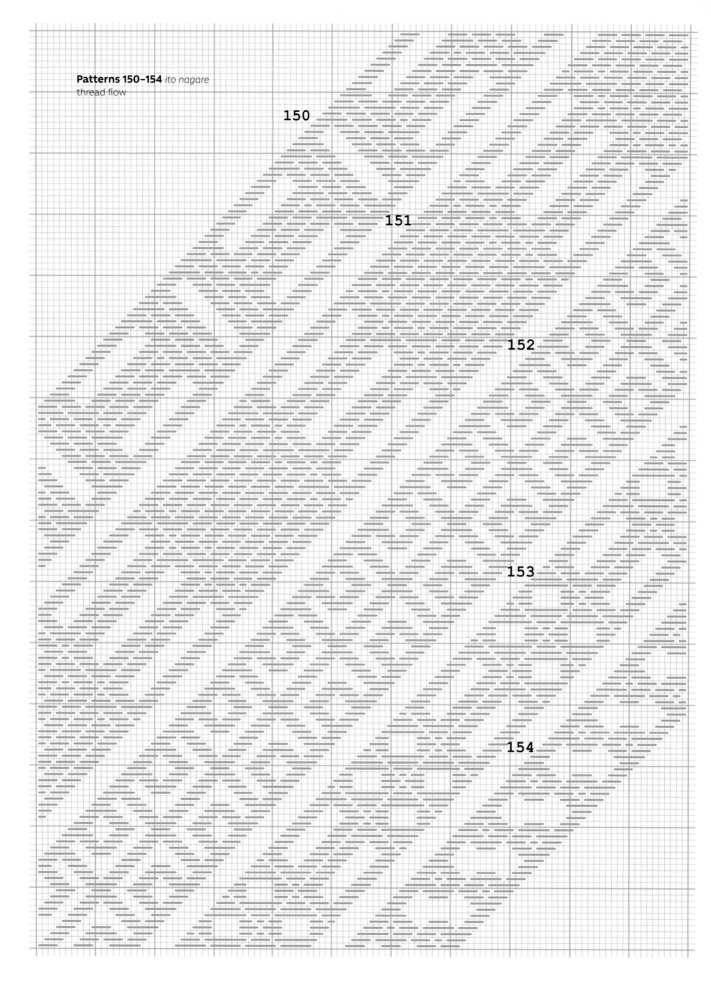

Patterns 150–154 *ito nagare*
thread flow

150

151

152

153

154

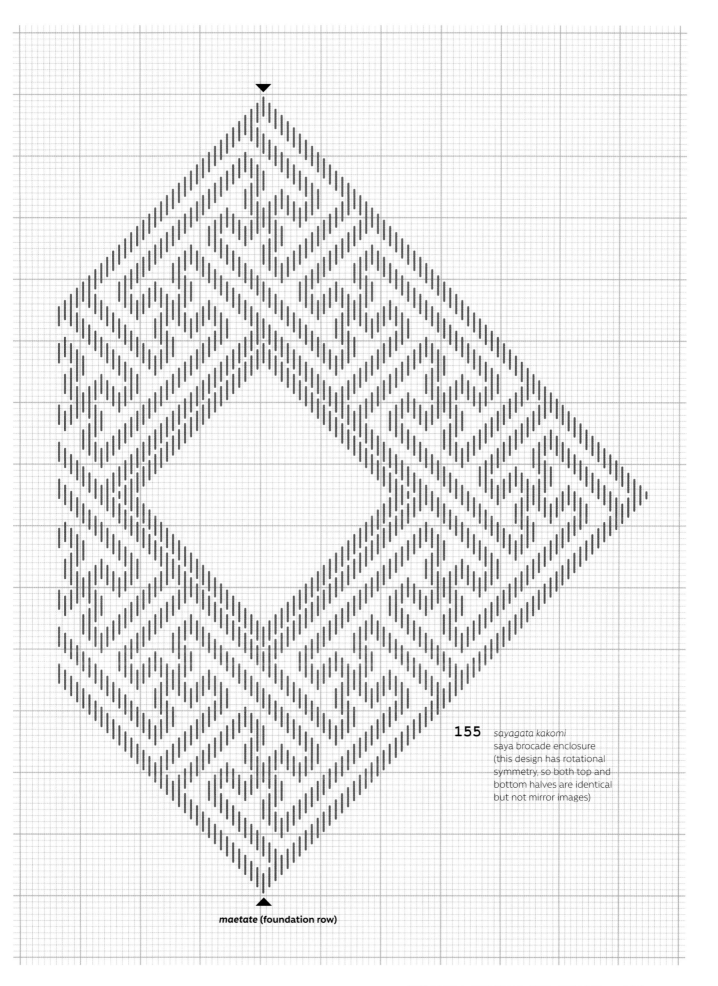

155 *sayagata kakomi*
saya brocade enclosure
(this design has rotational
symmetry, so both top and
bottom halves are identical
but not mirror images)

***maetate* (foundation row)**

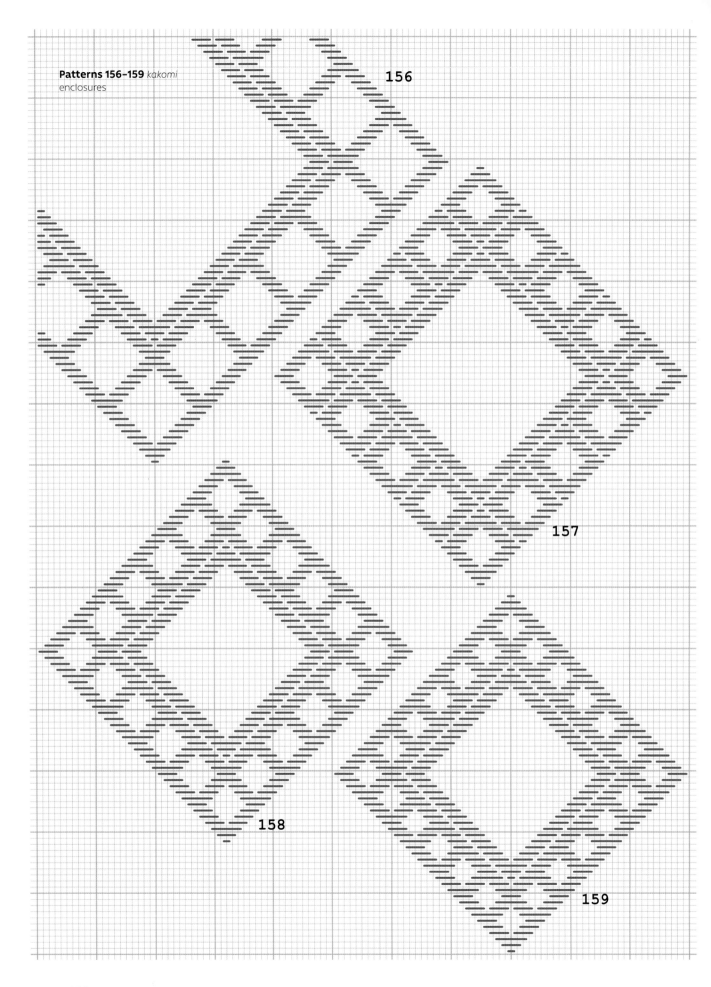

156

157

158

159

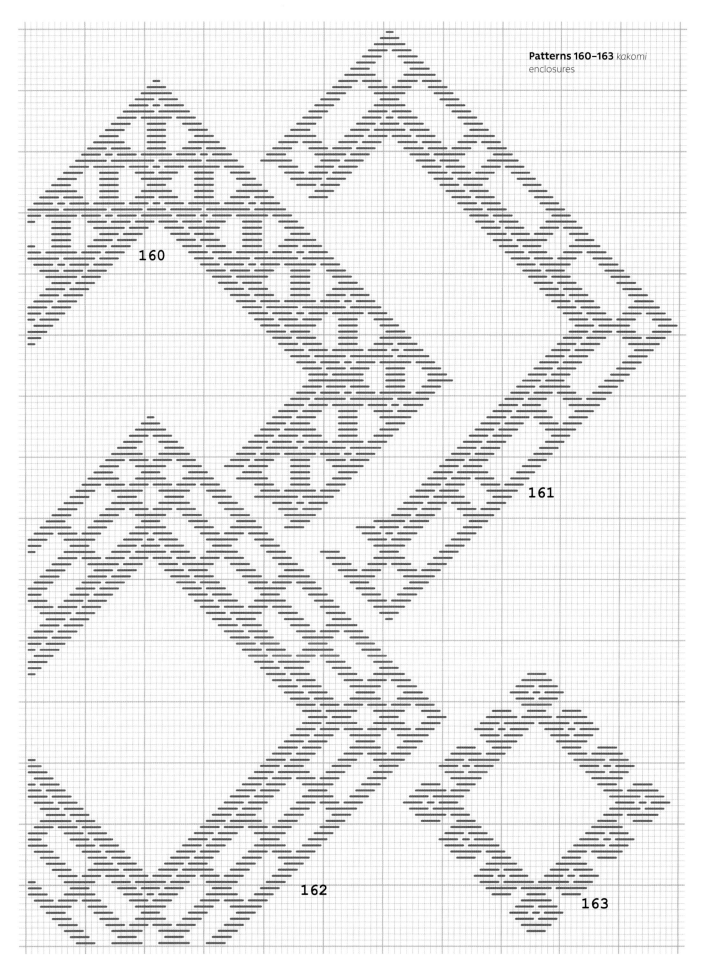

160

161

162

163

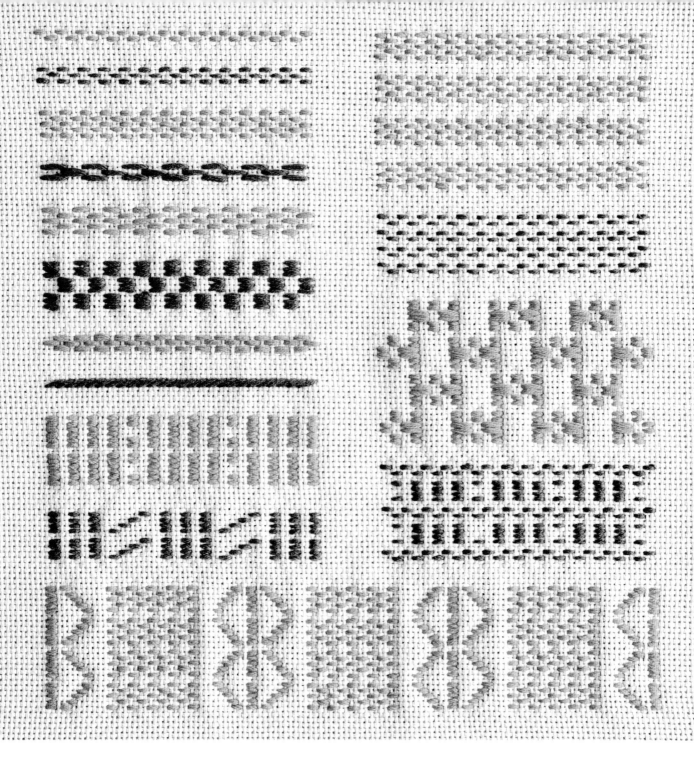

HORIZONTAL BORDERS

Unlike most other Higashi, Nishi and Mishima kogin patterns, many of these horizontal border patterns have stitches worked over two threads, rather than one or three. They were traditionally used at the bottom of jacket bodices where the obi sash would hide them. In the Nishi and Mishima traditions, the simplest borders were used to separate wide bands of kogin patterns on the bodice. Borders with stitches over two threads only have very short stitches on the right side of the work, so these patterns would have been very hard-wearing. Most do not have individual names and are known collectively as *take no fushi* (bamboo joint). Many of the stitches on the stitched sample are worked over just two threads, and pattern 173 is worked in stem stitch stepped over two rows, which creates an attractive corded effect.

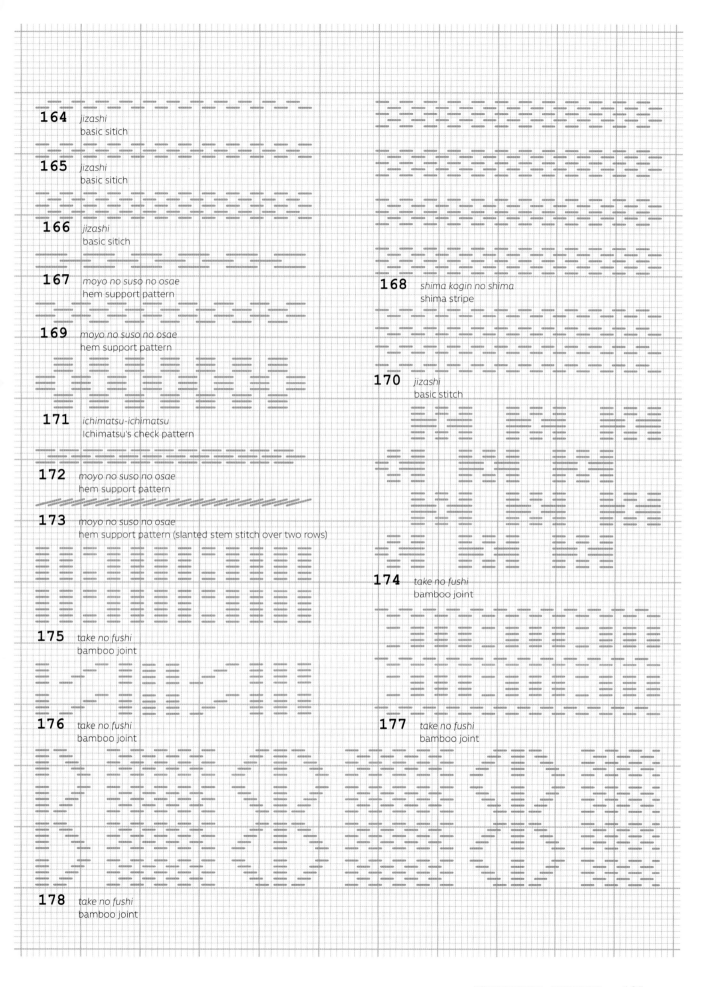

164 *jizashi*
basic sitich

165 *jizashi*
basic sitich

166 *jizashi*
basic sitich

167 *moyo no suso no osae*
hem support pattern

168 *shima kogin no shima*
shima stripe

169 *moyo no suso no osae*
hem support pattern

170 *jizashi*
basic stitch

171 *ichimatsu-ichimatsu*
Ichimatsu's check pattern

172 *moyo no suso no osae*
hem support pattern

173 *moyo no suso no osae*
hem support pattern (slanted stem stitch over two rows)

174 *take no fushi*
bamboo joint

175 *take no fushi*
bamboo joint

176 *take no fushi*
bamboo joint

177 *take no fushi*
bamboo joint

178 *take no fushi*
bamboo joint

Patterns 179–181 *take no fushi*
bamboo joint

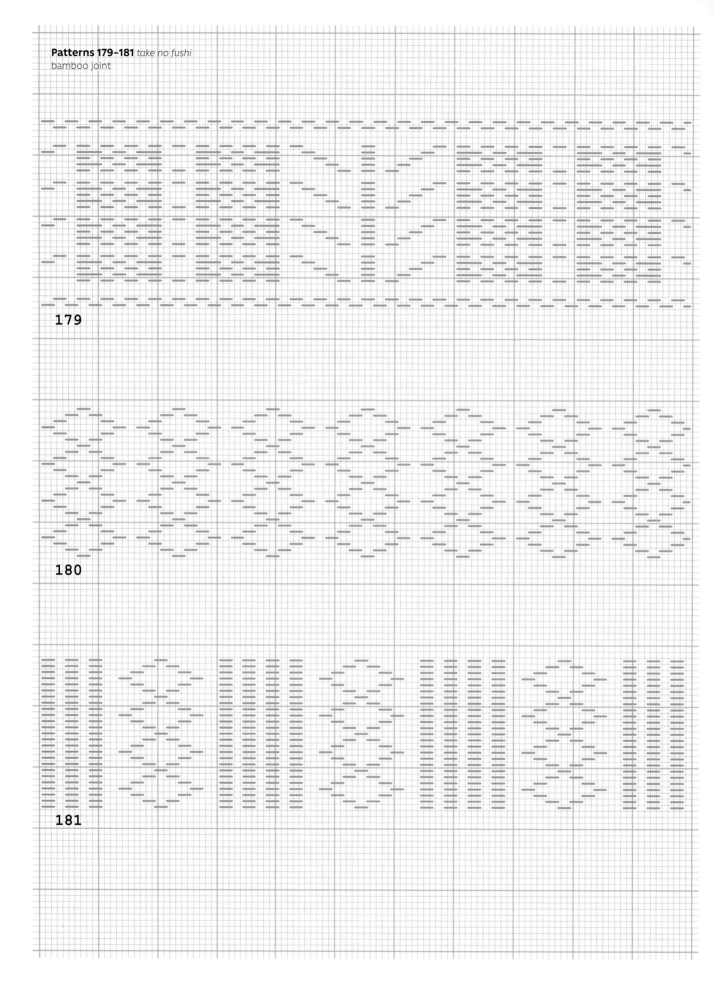

179

180

181

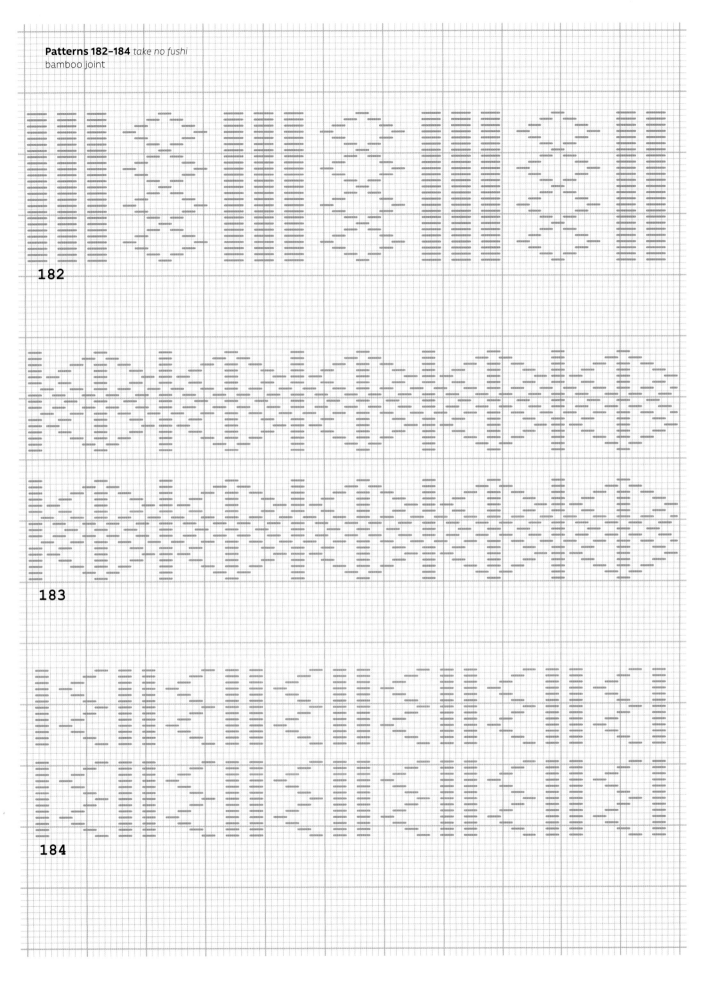

182

183

184

Patterns 185–187 *take no fushi*
bamboo joint

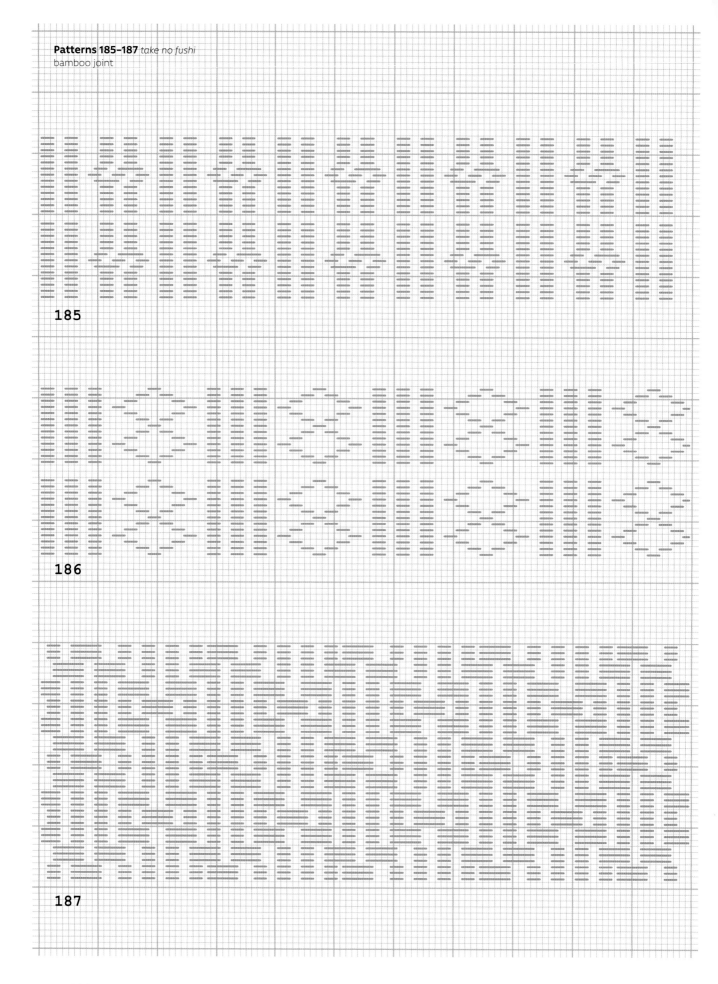

185

186

187

Patterns 188–191 *take no fushi*
bamboo joint

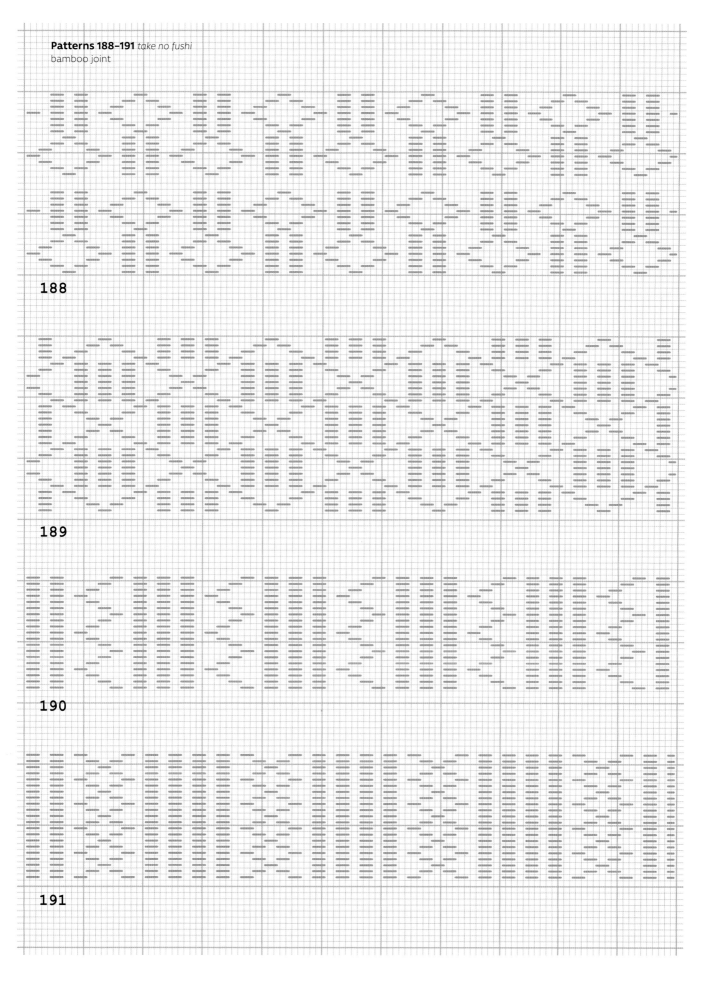

188

189

190

191

NANBU HISHIZASHI MOTIFS

Originating in the Nanbu area of Aomori Prefecture, these hishizashi (diamond stitch) patterns are worked over an even number of threads. Patterns sharing the same number of threads were used together (see Basic Techniques: Designing Kogin) and, on traditional Nanbu hishizashi aprons, changing the thread colours used created additional zigzag, diamond and diagonal hashtag or *igeta* (well curb) motifs (see Introduction: The Origins of Nanbu Hishizashi). On the central panels of Nanbu hishizashi aprons, the pattern edges were filled in with simple zigzag lines as seen in the stitched sample. Some stitches are worked over ten threads, which makes them rather long when worked on 18-count fabric as shown. For items that will receive a lot of wear, choose a higher thread count so these stitches are shorter.

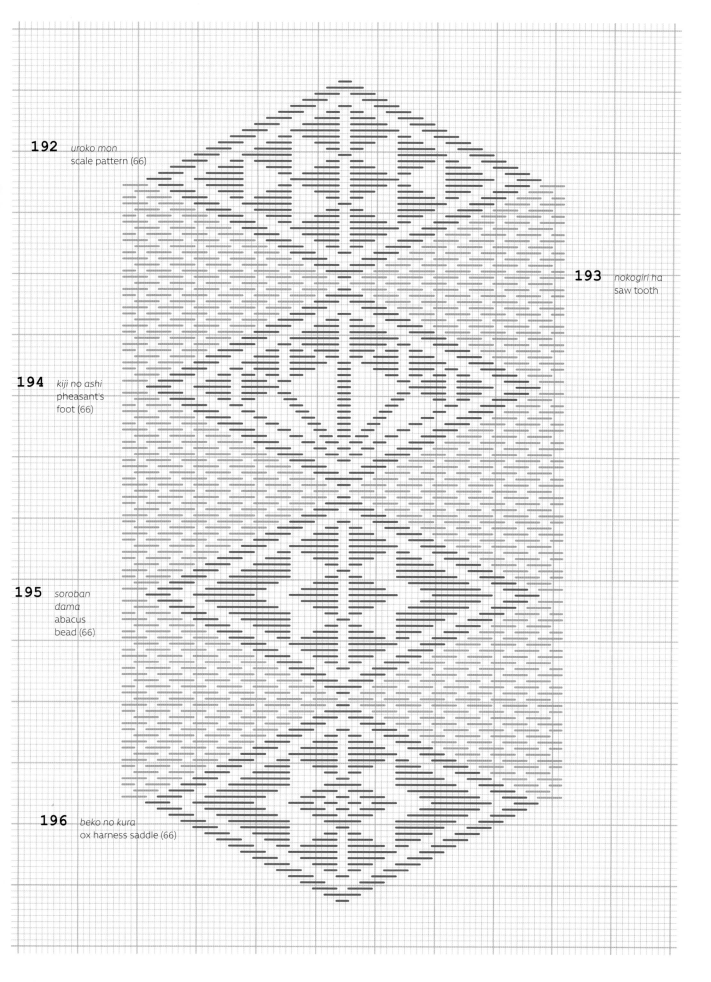

192 *uroko mon*
scale pattern (66)

193 *nokogiri ha*
saw tooth

194 *kiji no ashi*
pheasant's
foot (66)

195 *soroban
dama*
abacus
bead (66)

196 *beko no kura*
ox harness saddle (66)

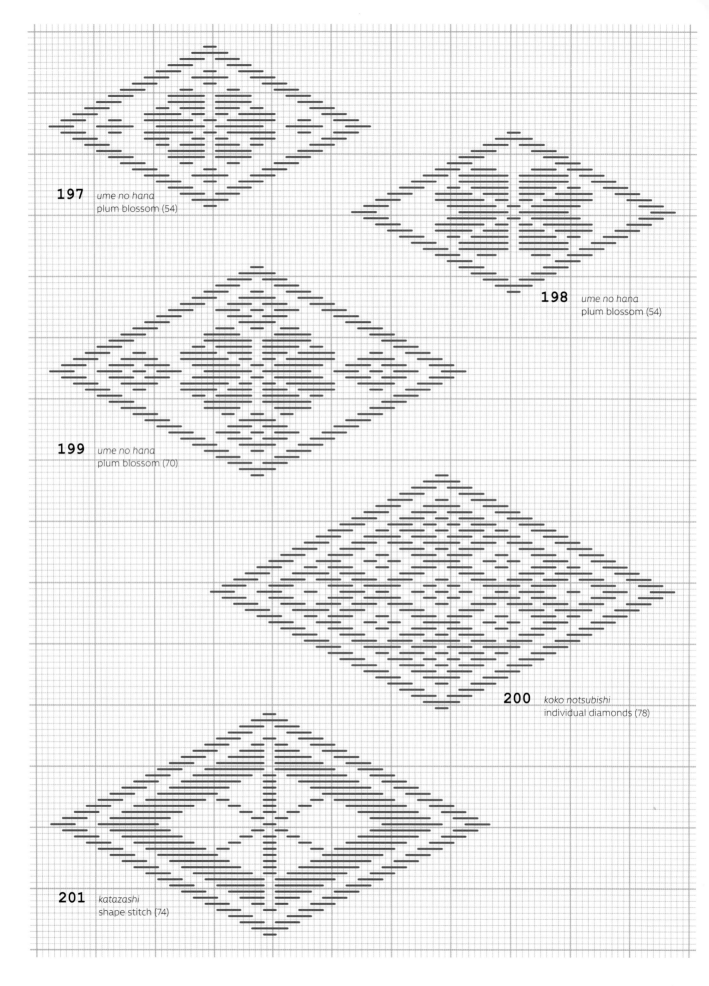

197 *ume no hana*
plum blossom (54)

198 *ume no hana*
plum blossom (54)

199 *ume no hana*
plum blossom (70)

200 *koko notsubishi*
individual diamonds (78)

201 *katazashi*
shape stitch (74)

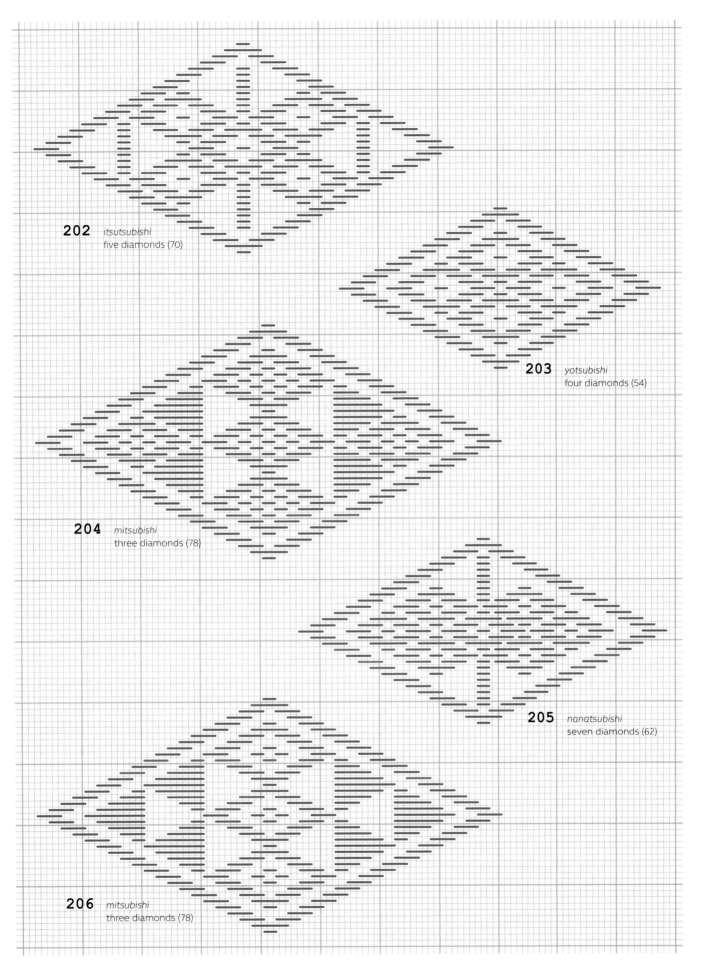

202 *itsutsubishi*
five diamonds (70)

203 *yotsubishi*
four diamonds (54)

204 *mitsubishi*
three diamonds (78)

205 *nanatsubishi*
seven diamonds (62)

206 *mitsubishi*
three diamonds (78)

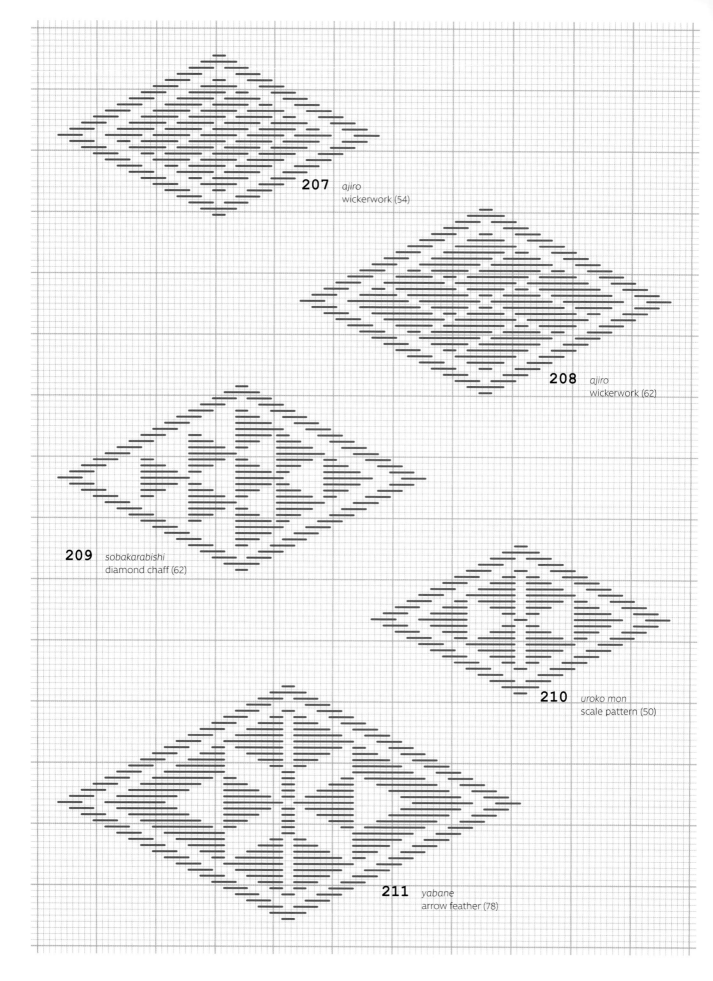

207 *ajiro*
wickerwork (54)

208 *ajiro*
wickerwork (62)

209 *sobakarabishi*
diamond chaff (62)

210 *uroko mon*
scale pattern (50)

211 *yabane*
arrow feather (78)

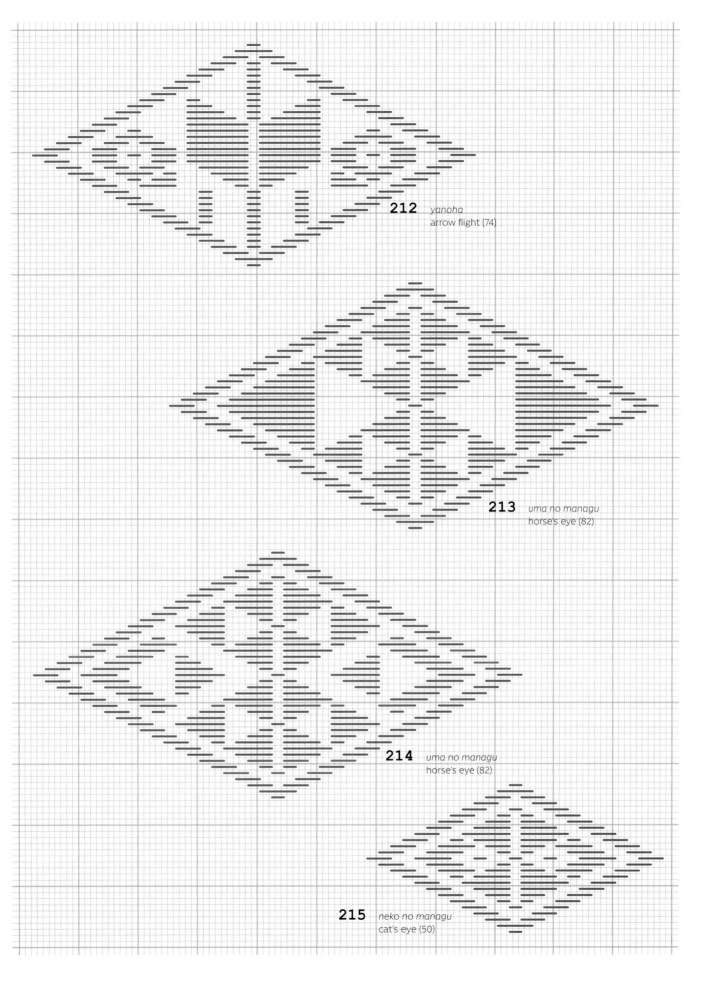

212 *yanoha*
arrow flight (74)

213 *uma no managu*
horse's eye (82)

214 *uma no managu*
horse's eye (82)

215 *neko no managu*
cat's eye (50)

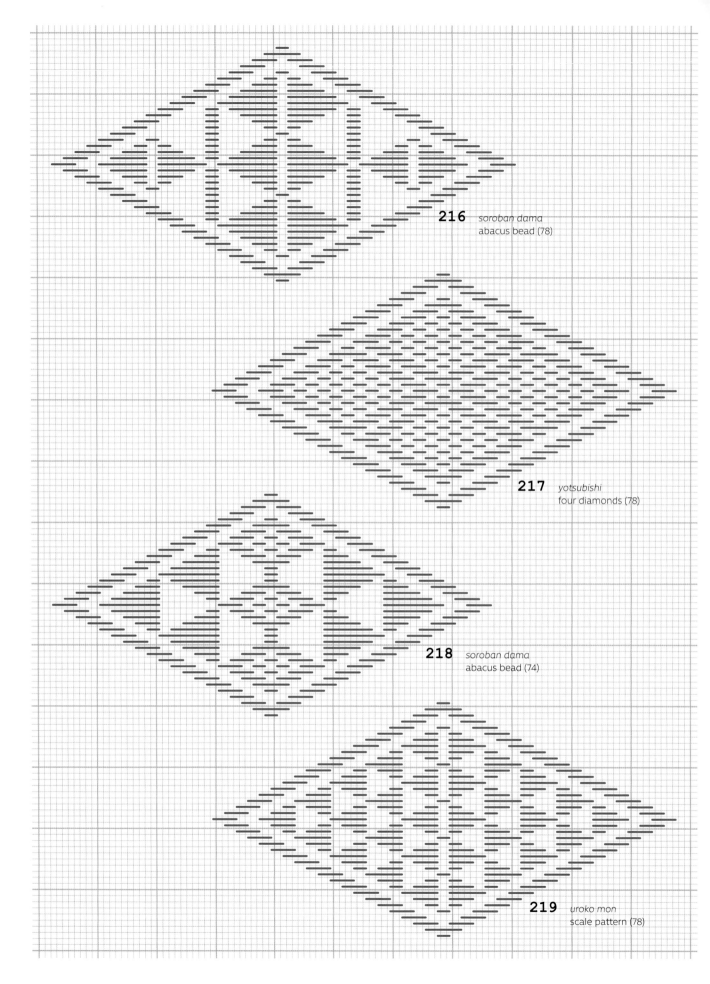

216 *soroban dama*
abacus bead (78)

217 *yotsubishi*
four diamonds (78)

218 *soroban dama*
abacus bead (74)

219 *uroko mon*
scale pattern (78)

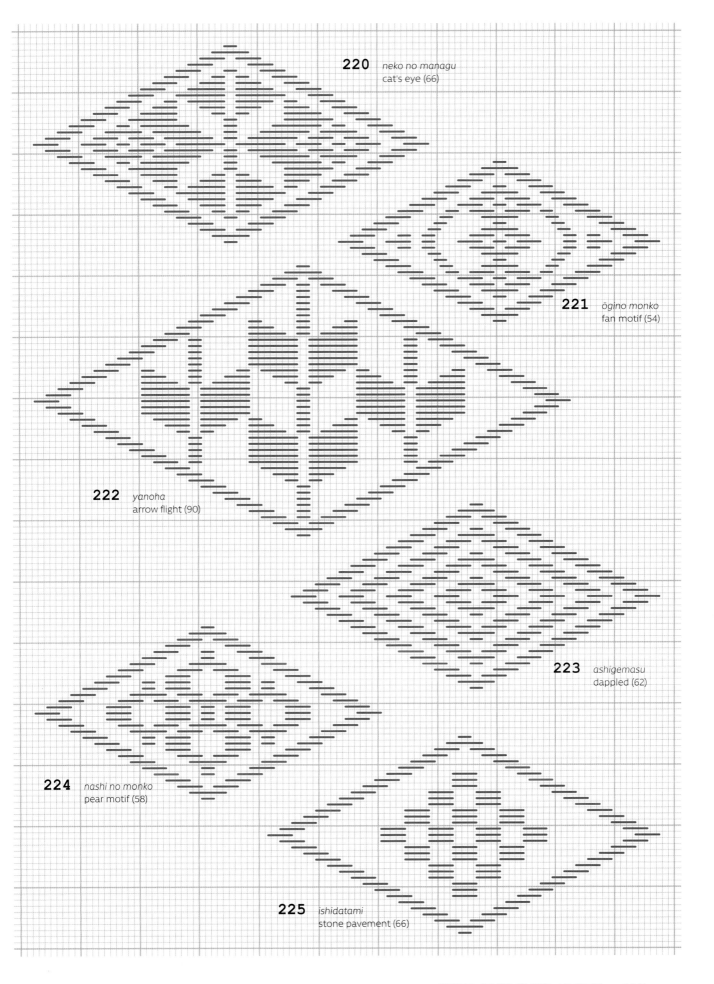

220 *neko no managu*
cat's eye (66)

221 *ōgino monko*
fan motif (54)

222 *yanoha*
arrow flight (90)

223 *ashigemasu*
dappled (62)

224 *nashi no monko*
pear motif (58)

225 *ishidatami*
stone pavement (66)

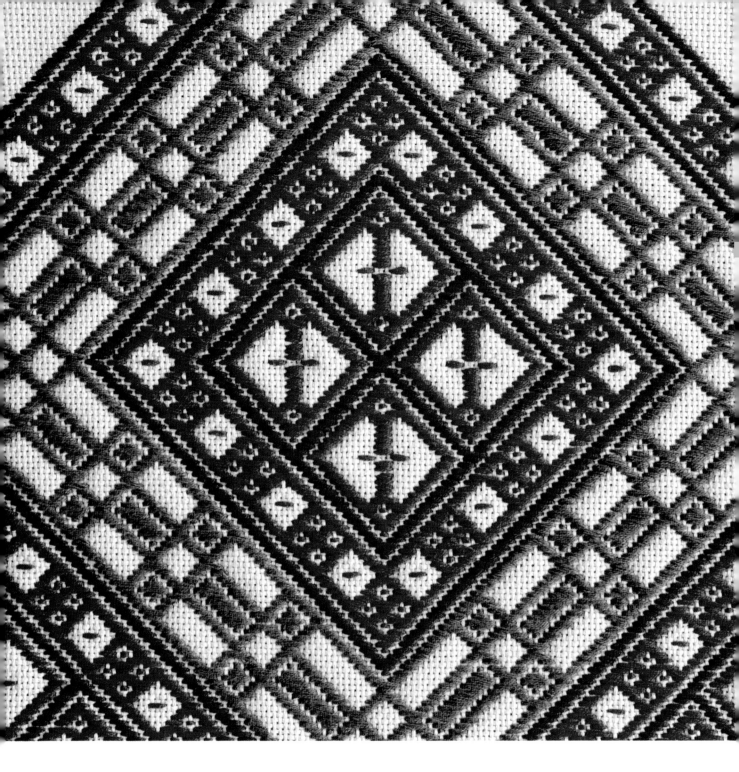

LARGE PATTERNS

The most complex patterns in kogin are made from combinations of patterns from all the previous sections in the Pattern Library. They are adapted from all three regional kogin traditions. Antique kogin often reveals areas where stitchers 'fudge' the patterns to make them fit one inside the other by shortening or lengthening sections in diagonal patterns or frames. Traditionally, large patterns covered the fabric side to side, but single large square-on-point motifs are popular today. Design your own large pattern combinations using graph paper (see Basic Techniques: Designing Kogin). In the stitched sample, individual patterns and frames are stitched in different colours to show the composition, but traditionally the whole design would have been stitched in one colour only.

226 Adapted from a large continuous pattern charted by Hirosaki Kogin Lab.

227 Adapted from a large continuous pattern charted by Hirosaki Kogin Lab.

228 Charted from the central motif in an all-over pattern on a Nishi kogin jacket, collection of Aomori City Council (former Keikokan Museum collection).

top

maetate (foundation row)

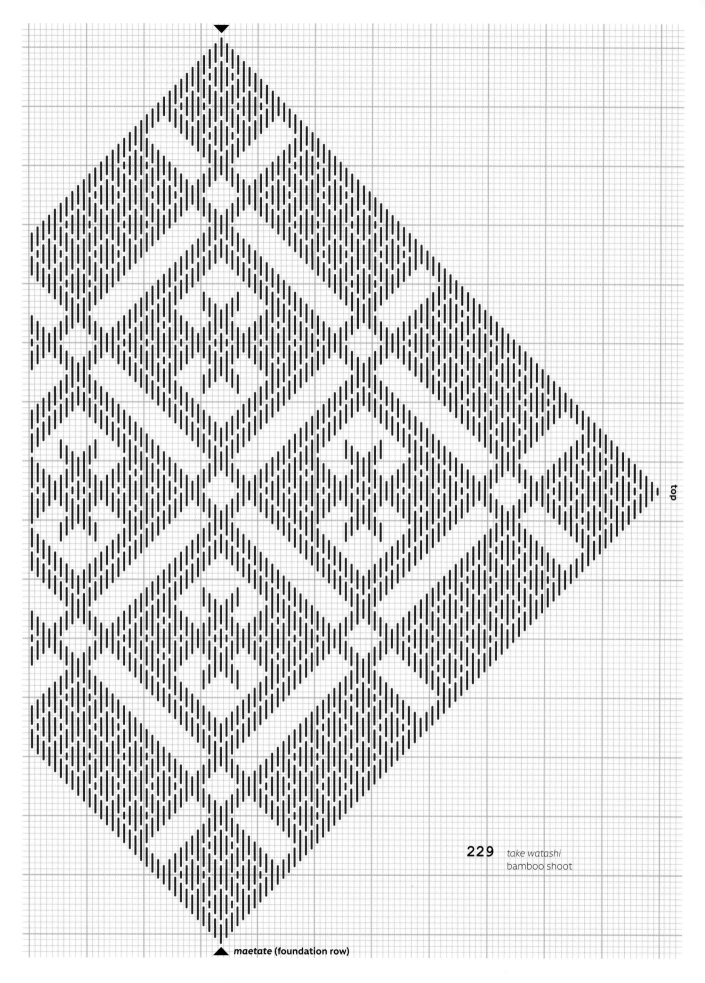

▼ top

229 *take watashi*
bamboo shoot

▲ *maetate* (foundation row)

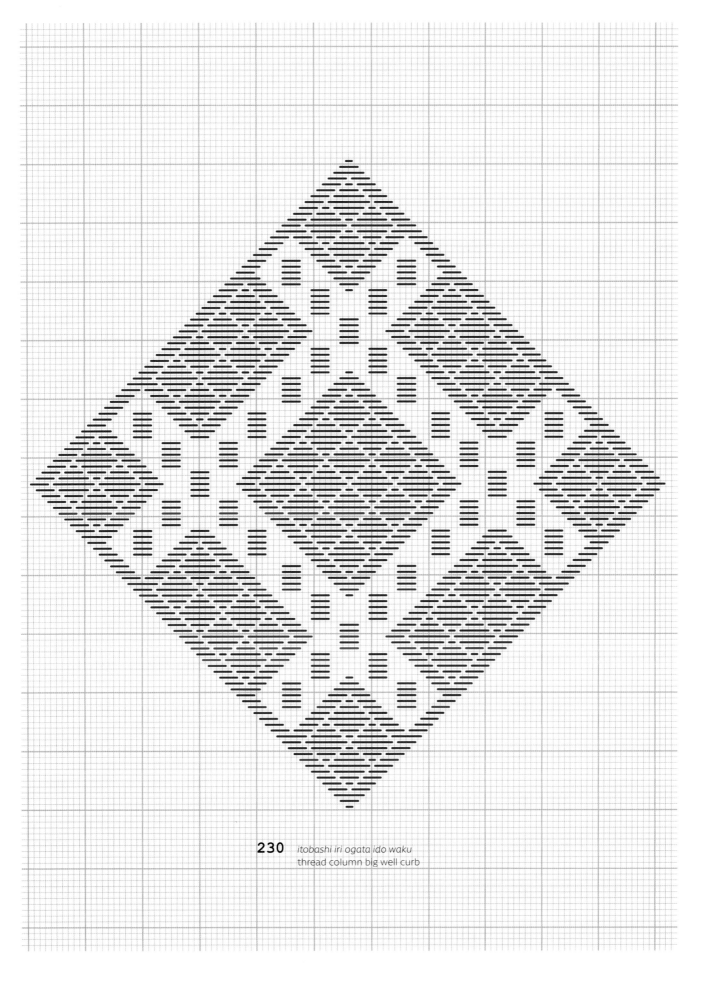

230 *itobashi iri ogata ido waku*
thread column big well curb

231   Adapted and charted from a Higashi kogin jacket, collection of Japan Folk Crafts Museum, Tokyo.

BIBLIOGRAPHY

Unfortunately not all of the following titles are available as English translations, and some may no longer be in print; I have provided ISBN details, which should help your internet searches.

► *Kogin and Sashiko Stitch*, Ogikubo Kiyoko (Kyoto Shoin, 1993, ISBN-13: 978-4763670489)

► *Kogin Zashi no Hon – Tsugaru no mingei shishū, Nuno-gei-ten*, Fukuda Rika & Tabanematsu Yōko (Bunka Shuppan Kyoku, 2009, ISBN-13: 978-4579112654)

► *Koginsashi zuan-shū 165 patān – dentō no koginsashi*, Hiroko Takagi (Mako Co., 2009, ISBN-13: 978-4837703099)

► *Shin Kogin Shishū Nyūmon*, Kimura Misao (Mako Co., 1991, ISBN-13: 978-4837715917)

► *The Unknown Craftsman: A Japanese Insight Into Beauty*, Sōetsu Yanagi & Bernard Leach (Kodansha, 2013, ISBN-13: 978-1568365206)

► *Tohoku no Sashiko* (Nihon Vogue Co., 2016, ISBN-13: 978-4529055949)

► *Tsugaru Kogin Zashi*, Hirosaki Kogin Lab (Seibundō Shinkō Sha, 2013, ISBN-13: 978-4416613900)

► *Zoku koginsashi zuan-shū 118 patān*, Hiroko Takagi & Kyoichi Harako (Makō-sha, 2013, ISBN-13: 978-4837701132)

Below is a list of additional publications and internet sources that I referenced in the writing of this book:

► *Hishizashi Moyō-shū*, Aiko Hatta & Tomiko Suzuki (Nihon Vogue Co., 1989 (reprinted 2017))

► *Kogin*, Naomichi Yokozima (Aomori Mingei Kyōkai, 1966)

► *Kogin Toge Shisū* (vol 1), Kikuko Miyake (Ondori Sha, 1959)

► *Kogin Toge Shisū 2*, Kikuko Miyake (Ondori Sha, 1960)

► *Kogin Toge Shisū 3*, Kikuko Miyake (Ondori Sha, 1967)

► *Kogin Toge Shisū*, Misao Kimura (Kodansha, 1965)

► *Tsugaru Kogin*, Naomichi Yokoshima (NHK, 1974)

► *Tsugaru Kogin Zashi*, Setsu Maeda (Tsukiya Inc., 1983)

► *Tsugaru Kogin Zashi*, Setsu Maeda (Nihon Vogue Co., 1981)

► *Tsugaru Kogin Sekai Shugei no Tabi 2* (Nihon Vogue Co., 1981)

► www.tohoku-standard.jp/en/standard/aomori/koginzashi/

► www.koginbank.com/about/kogin-zashi-hishi-zashi/

► www.koginlab.jimdo.com/home/patterns-and-meanings/

► www.jtex.wordpress.com/200%⅝5/kogin-historical-overview-1/

► www.acac-aomori.jp/category/acacblogen/2013aomori-gestures-in-clothing/

► www.komakino.jp/tugaru/teizo.html

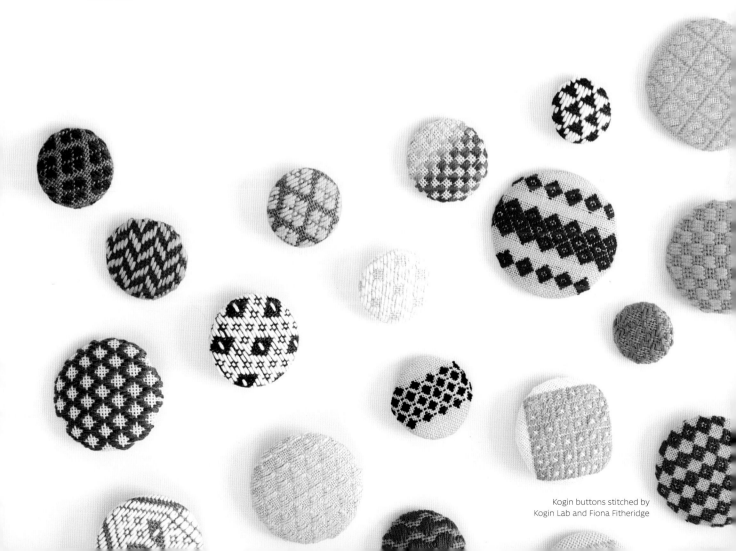

Kogin buttons stitched by
Kogin Lab and Fiona Fitheridge

SUPPLIERS

UK

Japan Crafts
www.japancrafts.co.uk

Susan Briscoe Designs
www.susanbriscoe.com

Out of Africa
For hand dyed threads
www.outofafricaquilts.co.uk

21st Century Yarns
For hand dyed threads
www.21stcenturyyarns.com

Sparklies
For hand dyed threads and evenweave fabric
www.sparklies.co.uk

FRANCE

Milpoint
Olympus Thread distributor
www.milpoint.com

SWEDEN

Marita Rolin
www.maritarolin.se

USA

Shibori Dragon
www.shiboridragon.com

Kimonomomo
www.kimonomomo.etsy.com

CANADA

A Threaded Needle
www.athreadedneedle.com

AUSTRALIA

BeBe Bold
www.bebebold.com

CHINA

Tianjin Zhaocheng Trade Co., Ltd
www.cnclover.com

JAPAN

Tsukiya
Hirosaki shop & mail order in Japan
ja-jp.facebook.com/tsukiya.kogin/

Yuzawaya
www.yuzawaya.co.jp

Craft Heart Tokai
www.crafttown.jp

Dream
www.dream-ono.co.jp

Okadaya
www.okadaya.co.jp

HONG KONG

Cheer Wool Co. Ltd
www.cheerwool.com

TAIWAN

Long Teh Trading Co., Ltd
www.patchworklife.com.tw

ABOUT THE AUTHOR

Susan Briscoe is a leading expert in traditional Japanese sewing techniques. She was first introduced to sashiko in the early 1990s while teaching English in northern Japan where she learned the technique and studied the history of patchwork and quilting. Susan has published numerous books about sashiko and is regularly featured in patchwork and quilting magazines.

ACKNOWLEDGEMENTS

I would like to thank the following people for their help in planning and creating this book:

Keiko Kawamoto of Olympus for meeting us in Hirosaki and for Japanese translation support; Olympus Thread Mfg. Co. for materials sponsorship; all our friends who helped in Hirosaki – Sadaharu Narita and his team at Kogin Lab; Yutaka and Ryo Sato; Yoko Satoh (for showing us her wonderful kogin collection); Takashi Takeuchi and his staff at *Tsukiya* needlework shop; the Maeda family; Toshiaki Takana and all the enthusiastic kogin experts and stitchers we met at the 7th Kogin Fes; Kiyoshi Tatsumi and the Amuse Museum, Tokyo; Fiona Fitheridge, who stitched the buttons, spiral panel and green border sampler; Katie Becker of Japan Crafts and Emily Creasey for travelling with me to Hirosaki; Keiko Abe for first teaching me the basics of kogin; my husband Glyn.

INDEX

A SEWANDSO BOOK
© F&W Media International, Ltd 2019

SewandSo is an imprint of F&W Media International, Ltd
Pynes Hill Court, Pynes Hill, Exeter, EX2 5AZ, UK

F&W Media International, Ltd is a subsidiary of F+W Media, Inc
10151 Carver Road, Suite #200, Blue Ash, OH 45242, USA

Text and Designs © Susan Briscoe 2019
Layout and Photography © F&W Media International, Ltd 2019

First published in the UK and USA in 2019

ISBN-13: 978-1-4463-0732-8 paperback
SRN: R9384 paperback

ISBN-13: 978-1-4463-7785-7 PDF
SRN: R9951 PDF

ISBN-13: 978-1-4463-7784-0 EPUB
SRN: R9950 EPUB

Printed in China by RR Donnelley for:
F&W Media International, Ltd
Pynes Hill Court, Pynes Hill, Exeter, EX2 5AZ, UK

10 9 8 7 6 5 4 3 2 1

Content Director: Ame Verso
Acquisitions Editor: Sarah Callard
Managing Editor: Jeni Hennah
Project Editor: Cheryl Brown
Design Manager: Anna Wade
Design: Sam Staddon
Art Direction: Sarah Rowntree
Photographer: Jason Jenkins
Illustrator: Kuo Kang Chen
Production Manager: Beverley Richardson

F&W Media publishes high quality books on a wide range of subjects.
For more great book ideas visit: www.sewandso.co.uk

Layout of the digital edition of this book may vary depending on reader hardware and display settings.